Neurons for Robots
A Tool Set

ISNB 1449599540
EAN-13 9781449599546

Keywords.
Robots, algebra, brains, computers, data, math, networks, neurons, nodes, HalNodes, HalTrees, systems

Also by Harold L. Reed

<u>Comparison and Choice</u>
About finding the least brain function.

<u>From Electric Numbers to Hal Trees</u>
5 ideas leading to Hal Trees

<u>Some Short Proofs of Fermat's Last theorem</u>
An application of Hal Algebra.

Neurons for Robots
A Tool Set

By
Harold L. Reed

Table of Contents

Table of Figures

1. To Open

On January 25, 1921 Karel Capek's play R.U.R (Rossum's Universal Robots), coined the name robot. In the play, robots were mechanical workers. The name caught on because it named a concept already established, that of animating lifeless objects. The name has been used in other fiction and some machines were beginning to be made that were named robots. This history is well known and I will not repeat it here, since we are not using any of it. Nor will I comment on current robotics research. The name robot has been misused ever since its origin on such things as welding arms and radio controlled machines. There have been many robots of all kinds built as artistic endeavors. Each of these has been unique, born with enthusiasm, and dying alone, their fifteen minutes of fame is all they ever get.

There is a reason for that, as there is a reason for almost everything. The main reason is there has been no common system to design robots with a common language. A common language is required for evolution to occur. No clever design could be transferred to another machine. It is hard to build anything when you have to build your tools first. Even invention of the simple computer required waiting for Claude Shannon (1916-2001) to marry Boolean algebra to switching circuits, making a language to write the instructions that built the computer with the switching circuits. There has been no such thing for robots and robots are different in kind from computers. If a computer is a line, a robot is a hypercube.

Now there is a language to build Robot brains and here it is in this book.

My interest in this arose because I like machines and brains are the most interesting machines on this planet. Like everyone else with that interest, I started with artificial intelligence ideas in 1958 and stuck with those ideas until 1976 when I was trying to make a computer program that could read. That did not work and I was old enough then to be able to discard AI and all of the experts and start looking on my own. What I began looking for was the least brain function and its mechanism. It had to be something that was simple and brainless that could be hooked up in networks of any scale and not to have any scale of its own.

What I discovered was an algebra of Hal streams. On 3/26/1994, I invented the C node while stumbling around in a forest of bit logic. That was the end and beginning. The time from 1958 to 1994 was not all work on this least brain search, I did have to work for a living, but technology had to produce the microprocessor and other key ideas before my solution became possible. I could have passed it by and it would have rested another hundred years, because it is so absurdly simple.

There are no tree structures in mathematics that match neuron and brain trees, so I had to invent a proper tree structure, built upward from two input nodes.

I began to think of nature as a set of calculating machines, as constrained by the rules of arithmetic as we are. I had invented a tool, and the universe was the nail for this hammer. I used the notions of switching algebra as background and reference. I made nodes and the cables to connect them. The algebra mapped directly to the hardware just like Boolean algebra matched logic gates. Like logic, there is a basic set of arithmetic that builds everything. Subtraction is the only operation of arithmetic that does exclusive or operations. You can build a complete arithmetic with subtraction and an inverter, just like you can build any logic system with AND and NOT gates.

I also abandoned logic as a design tool. Logic is a primitive language, suitable for building simple machines like computers and telephone switches and such but it is not nearly powerful enough to build any brain, which is why you only see four function robots.

From the axioms of brain, I will deduce some functions and make hardware and a coding system that I call Hal algebra, a language that maps exactly to robot hardware. In use, you write a program and that becomes the instructions to build a robot. The task of this book is to make the hardware for this language.

Once you have coded a robot, this code and hardware can be passed on to the next robot since brains are universal. Hal algebra is extendable to any degree.

I also have some ideas on how to build the bodies of robots, using the techniques of model building. That will be a chapter but I am more interested in the code to connect sensors to brains and brains to motors. In this book, everything is either a sensor or motor or brain Hal node. The connections are made with HalStreams, carried by ribbon cable.

Nature obeys the rules of arithmetic. We know from years of experimentation and study that physical actions always follow a path that consumes the least energy. Watch a bouncing ball. Jump off a building. That is how we must build Robots, to follow rules, goals and desires. To do that we must create a system of network algebra that can seek goals. We need to be able to build neurons. That is what you will learn to do. The hardest part will be getting rid of if-then logic and telling the machine what to do. Any brain function is far beyond logic, requiring goals to obtain and rules of action.

The reason robots have not propagated is simple. Designers have been trying to tell the machine what to do based on the value of its inputs. (If input is this then do that.) You have to get over that, since it simply does not work for large numbers of inputs. Input combinatorial complexity swamps all but simple machines. I knew that in 1960, but it still took until 1994 for me to get rid of it. Nature tells the machine what to do. You provide the goal seeking structures so that can happen. This book will give you the tools to handle the complexity. We will turn everything into numbers, as Pythagoras wanted to do. With numbers you can calculate. We will produce an algebra for thought. Once you learn this system, you will gain a new view of the world. I hope this book will give you that. It is wonderful.

Using this tool set, you and I will build the brains for some robots, starting with the simplest and ending with a human type robot.

1. Nature, environment, brain.

We live in a universe that is outside us. To react to this universe we need something to sense it and touch it. Before there was a brain, there were sensors to read the environment and motors to act on the environment. Call the environment E and we have a sensor, motor variable. E is outside. Sensors and motors let inside see and touch outside.

To us, nature is data. We read data, process them and produce new data for nature in a continuous loop.

How does nature become data? We must start with the simplest thing asking: does some event exist at some point? We make a pixel like thing that has properties, one of which is existence. So, as a number, we must be at least binary. There can be other properties that can be captured in this number and every property will add another bit to our pixel.

Let our pixel be S. Now, replicate S in one direction for X times to produce a line. The line has properties of size, dimension and base. Dimension is 1, size is X and base is S^X. Call this line number L. One number indicates a point on the line.

Now replicate L in one direction Y times. We have a new number with size Y, dimension 2 and base L^Y. Call this number P. Two numbers indicate a point in the flat surface.

Now replicate P in one direction for Z times. Now we have a cube with size Z, dimension 3 and base L^Z. Call this number C. Three numbers indicate a point.

Now replicate C in one direction A times. We have a new number with size A, dimension 4 and base C^A. Four numbers indicate a point.

This can be continued as far as you wish. Once you have a number base, you have every number in the system. For example in dimension 2 we can make every possible picture simply by enumerating the number P. This is also true of C and beyond. When we get beyond C we loose the picture, but still have the numbers that represent every n dimensional structure. N numbers indicate a point.

1. Sensor is a conversion function

A sensor is a neuron or machine that reads from nature, converts to a neuron or machine code and continually writes to a brain neuron or machine.

O = S(E) where S is the sensor function and E is the environment. The sensor detects and WRITES. Each sensor looks at only one aspect of E, so we must have many sensors of different kinds. The kinds of sensors depend on the task. Sensors are restricted by mathematical and physical restrictions and limitations.

Later on, we will go inside a sensor.

1. Motor pushes on nature

A motor reads data from a single brain neuron and converts it into a motion that works on E.

E = M(I) where M is the motor function and I is data from a brain neuron. A motor READS data and performs an action.

The engineering task is to determine the motor types and functions and to apply that to hardware for robots. There must be many kinds of motors for different tasks. Motors are limited in the same way sensors are, but for a different job. Motors can be divided into parts. The neuron or machine driver remains, but the motor action is muscle pull that requires a different cell type. The ensemble is still a motor by definition, since the assembly READS.

1. Brain is a list of neuron functions

We know that brains are not cooling systems as Aristotle thought. Beyond that, a brain is a bunch of neurons. There are several facts we can use to make a mathematical definition of brain. Brain is generally used to describe the hardware of the brain. For the software, let us invent brain code. Then brain is neurons assembled according to brain code. The facts are:

1. Brains are of different sizes.
2. Brains are made of neurons.
3. Brains are between sensors and motors.

From fact 2, we can deduce that if we list all the neurons in a particular animal, we can call that aggregate a brain code.

Therefore, a brain code is a list of neuron functions. The neurons are hardware. The brain code, being a list, is software. If we make a list of neurons, we can call that a brain code. We leave loose the brain code list, so it can be used for pure brain neurons or the whole assemblage of sensors, motors and brain, which would include the entire robot.

Brain code is to neurons as a computer program is to a computer. The rest of this book will be working to learn how to make brain codes. It is no harder than learning to write computer codes. Note that brain code can describe brains that are smaller than a neuron.

The only animal I know of that has been completely catalogued to a parts list is the worm C. elegans. It has about 304 neurons, which must include sensor and motor neurons. I count about 14 motor neurons and about 86 sensor neurons. Subtract those from the total neurons and you have about 204 neurons. So the brain code for c. elegans would involve 14 functions of 89 sensors. If we could define each of the 14 functions, we would have the brain code for C. elegans. In any animal, if we count the sensors, brain and motor neurons, we can calculate the number of functions and the function sizes.

1. Neuron is a function

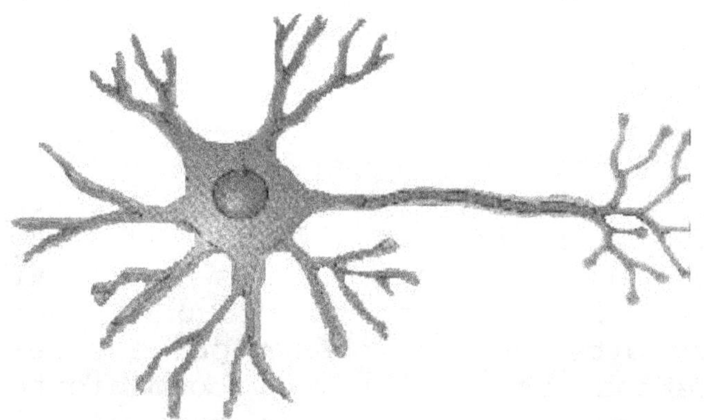

Figure 1 Neuron

Everyone has a different view of a neuron depending on the tools they use. Since they are cells, there are many different kinds of neurons as you would expect from functional considerations. It costs life forms very little to waste cells.

It is relatively easy to measure the electrical properties of neurons, so that, in turn, rapidly became the story on how they worked. Every description I have ever read about neurons states that neurons emit electrical signals that travel down the axon, repeating to form a pulse code. However, the only thing that reads this pulse code is the person doing the neuroscience. There is never any input of this electrical pulse. There is no question that this happens, but why, if there is no input for this output, is this required. The pulse code itself does not have enough range to compute with. Pulse codes are in the range of kilohertz in neurons. There are not many bits in a kilohertz pulse stream so I am sure that is not how they communicate.

As a mathematician, I am interested only in the connections, the synapses and function we can see. In simple animals, you can count the neurons and see the connections. In addition, people are more interested in the mechanics of neurons, their electrical properties, than in the data passed. People think they have thousands of connections. Let us look at them as HalTrees, to be defined later, and see how they would connect.

One truth we need to remember is that neurons connect to each other, except when connected to muscles or sensors. That means that input data and output data must be in the same form and data type. We need to determine the size of the data. Here is the data flow:

E -> sensors -> brain -> motors -> E

What this means is that the total possible connections must equal the number of neurons plus sensor connections minus muscle connections. In live neurons, unused synapses are removed. In robots, we remove inactive Hal Nodes.

What are the relevant facts about neurons that we need to consider.

1. Neurons have a single output called the axon.
2. Neurons have multiple inputs called synapses.
3. Neurons compute something.
4. Axon = f(all synapses)

With those four facts, we can build a neuron in a mathematical fashion. If you just look at a neuron you see a function. Synapses are domain and axon is range. Synapses are inputs and axon is output.

Any device with multiple inputs and a single output will combine into a HalTree. (Hal trees will be fully developed later. For now, imagine a tree with one trunk where the data comes in on the leaves and goes out the trunk.) If there is a HalTree, there is a minimum HalTree. A minimum HalTree is one with two inputs. We can postulate a two input neuron that is a neuron with two synapses and one axon. (Be assured that two input things can connect into any size tree.) Somewhere in nature, you might even find a two synapse neuron. Any microbe will fit this also. Take the worm C. elegans for a bigger example. It has about 304 neurons including sensor and motor neurons. There are 14 motor neurons and about 86 sensor neurons. Subtract those from the total neurons and you have 204 brain neurons. As we will find out, each motor neuron is a function so we can count neurons and sensor for each function. There are about 6 sensors per function, (86/14) so we could make a full two input HalTree with 15 HalNodes per function. We get 14.57 when we divide 14 into 204. So we are four neurons short. Considering that both motors and sensors are estimates, I think the point is proved. The neurons in C. elegans can average only two inputs or synapses each. They have to make some kind of tree and their backward fan out number is two. The state number of C. elegans is b^86. Let b = 8, that is every sensor can have 8 different outputs. Then C. elegans can have
8^86 = 4.6316835E77 different inputs to take action on. The functions in C. elegans average about 6 inputs each. This is a workable number of inputs. H = 2^6 we can write down. Each neuron gets only 64 binary inputs. The neuron reduces that to one output via inner function trees.

Assume two sensors, one excitatory and one inhibitory (taking words from brain folks.) Let us name the sensors Se and Si and name the muscle M. Then we have M = Se - Si which is a function. Now, keep this one neuron and increase the sensors, keeping half of them inhibitory. Then we have a tree of functions. Think of all neurons as being composed of trees of two input functions. We can do all this without knowing anything about the architecture of c. elegans brain.

1. What Functions are Possible

Axon = f(all synapses). What kinds of functions can a neuron compute? It is a tree and trees add their own functions to the basic functions. Let S+ be the excitatory synapses and S- be the inhibitory synapses. Let Sj and Sk be any synapses. Let A be the axon. Then A = f(S+, S-). So we are looking at two streams of data. So we can do arithmetic. We must have addition and subtraction before we can compare two functions.

Neurons make sensors, motors and brain functions. Let us call them sensors, brain and motors. Then we have a data flow that can be specified.

E -> sensors -> brain -> motors -> E

This is a loop. Sensors read E, write to brain. Brain reads sensors and writes to motors. Motors read brain and write to or push on E. So, a brain neuron is both motor and sensor, since it reads data, and writes data.

The task now is to determine some representative functions and to make them into hardware. Since we do not know actual neuron functions, we must develop them from mathematical necessity. What functions are allowed? Surely we can use arithmetic (+,-,*,/}. What about using logic (AND, OR and so on) for operators?

Neurons must obey the rules of mathematics and physics, and, since they are a cell, the biological rules of the cell.

We can make numbers representing the data flow of the neuron in many ways. A simple count of the number of each neurotransmitter is one number system. This treats each neuron as a digit in base b where b is the number of molecules.

It is certain that there is only one output at any time t, so if we establish a number for the axon, that is all we have to do. This would be nice to know, but we don't have to have it. We know it is a cyclic number and a single digit. We are looking for integer functions. We can make a model structure for the neuron with binary numbers. From that we can go upward to larger base.

A brain is a list of functions. Make each axon a variable. Write the functions. This is the brain construction list. This is before we know what the functions are. We know that neurons reduce the input complexity to a single digit. b^s -> b. The only mathematical structure that can do that is a HalTree.

There is some background math needed for this system. We need number base, digits, variables, sets, systems, and Hal trees as math objects. We can go on to develop a set of neuron functions from the bottom up, once those are defined.

I think the neuron is a single digit, but it could hook up with other neurons to be some kind of multi digit system although I don't think you will find any decimal points in nature. Anyhow, let us talk about digits.

1. Bits, Digits, logic and arithmetic

A variable is a named placeholder for an object. Think of it as a box with a name plate or a computer register or a spread sheet cell. The variable, the box remains regardless of its content. The variable's name remains while it is in consideration. Giving the variable a name is all that is needed to create it.

So, we make a variable. I will name it A. Now what can we put in A? What can you do with a single variable? You can count.

The smallest object we can put in a single variable is a single bit. The value of a bit is either 0 or 1. The count with a single bit is: 0 1 0 1 0 1 ... (The space between 0 and 1 represents successive values of the counting process. The three dots indicate we can continue this as long as we want.) A single variable is a digit. It has no carry mechanism.

A number has the properties of base and value. The numbers we are going to be dealing with are single digits of base b. First, we generalize digit to mean any set of symbols of the digit. Number base b for the digit then is simply a count of the symbols needed to express all the values it can have. For example: Binary digits have two symbols, 0 and 1. The base b of the binary digit is the symbol count of two. Base b = 3 is -1, 0 and 1, so we have three symbols.

Instead of a number line, with the digit, we have a number wheel. Every digit cycles on b and if we make a digit wheel it will have b clicks or spaces for symbols around the wheel. The base b can be any number from 0 to n, but it must be countable. The digits we will be using are base 256. Count is 0,1...255,0,1...

(We can make 256 symbols by reusing old symbols as we do with multi digit numbers. 255 here is one symbol, not 3 and not 2*5*5. All we need to do to use multi digit symbols is to use an explicit multiply symbol. Then any connected set of symbols can be treated as one symbol.)

Large variable names are required in large robots, but we know how to do that from the computer syntax requirements.

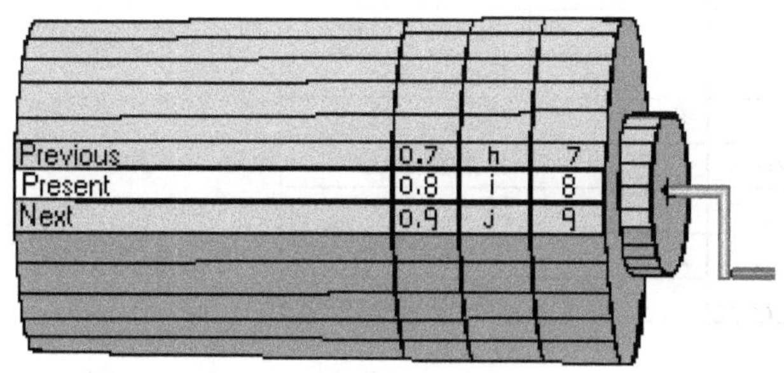

Figure 2 Digit Wheel with Clicker

Here is a picture of a number wheel with b clicks. Note that all the symbols of other systems are side by side here, not squeezed in as they are in the number line. (It is easy to prove that all numbers are digits, but that is in another book.)

The machines we are going to make are single digit cyclic just like neurons. The variables we are going to make use electric bit numbers.

A digit is a cyclic number of base b. Here are two digits with all their states shown:

digit1	count name	digit2	count name
0	zero	0	Sunday
1	one	1	Monday
2	two	2	Tuesday
3	three	3	Wednesday
4	four	4	Thursday
5	five	5	Friday
6	six	6	Saturday
7	seven	0	Sunday
8	eight	1	Monday
9	nine	2	Tuesday
0	zero	3	Wednesday

Digit1 is a familiar base 10 digit. All digits cycle like digit2, a base 7 digit. For all digits, the name count is the base. Notice that the base cannot be a name or state of the digit and that the last name + 1 is also the base. A digit base can be any counting number.

Let b = 12. Count
0,1,2,3,4,5,6,7,8,9,10,11,0...
We simply reuse the b symbols to create new symbols instead of new digits. Do that instead of:
0,1,2,3,4,5,6,7,8,9,ten,eleven,0...

Let b = 10,000
Count then is from 0 up to 9,999,0... and it is still one digit.

Let b = 3. Count 0,1,2,0...
Here is a table of b and symbols

b	symbols
0	0
1	1
2	0,1
3	0,1,2
4	0,1,2,3
5	0,1,2,3,4

To make digits real so they can be manipulated and seen, we make an electrical analog. Digits are carried on wires now.

Here is a table of wires with voltage names.

Wires	**names**	**capacity or usage**
1	P	none
2	P,G	Power, ground
3	P,G,S	Power, ground, signal
4	P,G,-P,S	Pwr,gnd,-pwr,signal

1 wire: Nothing can be done with one wire. No flow can be made.

2 wires: Connect two wires to a battery. With a good power supply, P - G = constant.

3 wires: P - G = K. S - G = variable. Now we can define the number S as gradations of P - G. If P - G = 9 then we can make numbers from 0 to 9, or 0 1 2 3 4 5 6 7 8 9 as gradation values. We have sort of a positive digit here. Computation can be done as long as we stick to all positive or all negative numbers. To fix that we need:

4 wires: Now numbers are graded by the distance between P and -P. Still V = S - G but now V can become negative. With this V, we can do almost any computation, including subtraction. Since we can do almost any computation, why did these analog numbers not take over? Why are you not using an analog personal computer?

The problem arises when P - G is not constant. If that happens, our number gradations go to pot. If the power supply is noisy, so is our number. This is not just a noise problem. When the P - G changes, our number base changes. Another problem is that of number size. Either large voltage differences or finer discrimination is required. Both of these requirements have problems.

The great advantage that analog numbers have is that they already flow because the defining electricity is a flow of electrons. Electrons flowing through a resistance create a voltage difference across the resister. That difference is our number. We have no number without electron flow.

To fix the P - G voltage change fault, we make the number definition worse and we go back to three wires.

The number is derived from S , but we define a new number B this way:
If S is near P then B = 1. If S is near G then B = 0.
There are just two gradations between P and G. That seems worse, but now P can vary a lot before the number will change from 1 to 0 or vice versa. We make B robust. The number size requirements go away. With base 2 numbers, one can do Boolean algebra.

Surely, this has fixed all the computational problems. It has certainly fixed all problems that can be solved by switching algebra.

Switching algebra was invented before the computer of course, since you could not have made a computer without it. Can we go up a step? Now that we have $5.00 computers, it is simple.

Keep all the electricity, all the switching algebra and add a simple expansion and a change in hardware. Instead of using base 2 digits, to compute, use a base that can do arithmetic. To make those from base 2 digits, simply parallel base two digits to make a digit of base = 2^{digits}. Use the notion of sensors writing a stream of digits to make digit flow. All the electricity is included in all the nodes. We end up with 10 wires(P,G,D7,D6,D5,D4,D3,D2,D1,D0) giving us a base 256 digit (2^8).

Then we go back to 4 wires, P, G, C, and D with power, ground control bit and data bit. The nodes do base 256 arithmetic but the number is carried bit serially over C and D. We trade time for space. We can now use any base we want to spend the time for. The data still flows over two wires. From here on, the numbers will be flowing electric and the operators will be computers. When you see a variable imagine numbers flowing into or out of it.

Variables are increased simply by naming another variable with another name. Simply create the variable B. Now we have two variables, A and B.

With one variable, we could count. With two variables, we can do arithmetic. We can add A to B and subtract B from A and so on. Now let us do this with one bit. Add A to B with one bit and there are these possibilities:

A	B	A+B	A-B	B-A
0	0	0	0	0
0	1	1	1	1
1	0	1	1	1
1	1	0	0	0

George Boole and others working with single bits realized you could not add and subtract them properly so they made a more primitive logical system of AND, OR, NOT instead of add and subtract. Add an exclusive or, XOR, > and < to that to complete the set.

A	**B**	**A and B**	**A or B**	**A xor B**	**Not A**
0	**0**	**0**	**0**	**0**	**1**
0	**1**	**0**	**1**	**1**	**1**
1	**0**	**0**	**1**	**1**	**0**
1	**1**	**1**	**1**	**0**	**0**

We can do the same with >, < and =

A	**B**	**A > B**	**A < B**	**A = B**
0	**0**	**0**	**0**	**1**
0	**1**	**0**	**1**	**0**
1	**0**	**1**	**0**	**0**
1	**1**	**0**	**0**	**1**

Note the only logic and arithmetic that match are subtract and XOR. Also, the operators make numbers them selves. AND is 1, > is 2, < is 4, XOR is 6 and OR is 7 in this arrangement. The operators as numbers can be manipulated as numbers.
AND + XOR = OR since 1 + 6 = 7.

Do them again, now naming the A,B pairs and making numbers of them.

A	B	Pair name
0	0	Z
0	1	L
1	0	G
1	1	E

The name of the pair 0 0 is Z
The name of the pair 0 1 is L

Now make a number from Z, L, G, and E and name the 4 bits.

```
Z L G E
0 0 0 0 Z       ;Z
0 0 0 1 AND     ;*,/,
0 0 1 0 GT      ;
0 0 1 1 GTE     ;"
0 1 0 0 LT      ;"
0 1 0 1 LTE     ;"
0 1 1 0 XOR     ;<>, - without borrow
0 1 1 1 OR      ;+ without carry
1 0 0 0 NOR     ;Not OR
1 0 0 1 NXOR    ;Not XOR
1 0 1 0 NLTE    ;Not LTE
1 0 1 1 NLT     ;Not LT
1 1 0 0 NGTE    ;Not GTE
1 1 0 1 NGT     ;Not GT
1 1 1 0 NAND    ;Not AND
1 1 1 1 NZ      ;Not Z
```

That is the complete set of logic operators. However, only these 4 are unique and useful for robots:

Z	L	G	E		
0	0	0	1	AND	A = B
0	0	1	0	GT	A > B
0	1	0	0	LT	A < B
1	0	0	0	NOR	A and B = 0

AND operator and the NOR operator survive from Boolean algebra. As far as I know Boole did not define GT and LT as logic operators. It requires a computer to make GT and LT operators and George Boole had no computer.

All the others can be made from these.
XOR = LT + GT = 0 1 1 0 = 4 + 2
OR = LT + GT + AND = 0 1 1 1 = 4 + 2 + 1
NAND = NOR + LT + GT = 1 1 1 0 = 8 + 4 + 2
and so on.

Now let us name another variable, so we have three, and make a new sign = (equals) and finally, we can do algebra. Create a new variable C to store the result of A and B. Then we can write and manipulate variables without caring about what they contain.

C = A + B; is a proper algebraic statement. It is also true that, regardless of anything else, A = C - B. A + B is just another name for C. For robots, one can also say that A + B causes C or A and B are inputs and C is output. Also, A + B precedes C in time.

Algebra works on logic also. It is the number three that creates algebra, not what its operators do. We now have a sort of number system of numbers and variables that we can make into a table.

Variables	What is possible
0	Nothing
1	Counting
2	Counting, Arithmetic, Logic
3	Counting, Arithmetic, Logic, Algebra

These are real limits. No matter how you push, one variable or one bit cannot do arithmetic.

1. Sets

2. Sets and containers

Mathematics is mostly about containers to hold actions or objects. We need containers because we must always limit the scope of our discourse, so we can know exactly what we are talking about. Variables are containers for numbers. A variable is an object. In the equation:

A = B - C

the = and - together are the actions of store and subtraction. A, B and C are the variables and the objects.

So, mathematical things are actions and objects. As variables contain numbers, sets contain variables or actions or anything we want to hold and contain. Variables are created by simply giving them a name.

Sets have a symbol that looks like a container. To create a set you put objects or actions or anything between brackets and give it a name, like this: ThisSet = {a, b, c}. The things within a set are variables or another set. They can be counted. Of course you can specify objects that are uncountable.
UC = {all variable names} ; is a perfectly legal set that cannot be counted, mainly because it is nonsense.

As in numbers, there is a zero set: null = {} which is a set with nothing in it. So sets replicate numbers on another scale.

Since a set can contain any object and a set is an object then a set can contain other sets.

1. Systems

2. General Systems

System is an old concept, but I am an old person so I retain the name. We need something that can contain both objects and actions and relate them to each other. The name is arbitrary.

A system is a coordinated set of actions and objects.

That means that with the container is a procedure or program that relates what actions do to objects.

Systems exist in nature and natural systems can be analyzed. Systems can be created at will. Systems are a container and isolator of our discourse. We are always in some kind of system and thus limited in what we can do. There is, of course a null system.

Null-System = {}, just like the null set.

Every System = {Actions, Objects}. The program that coordinates them is defined outside the system container. It might take a book to explain the program. We could give it a name in the brackets but instead use the system name to represent the program as well. The program also gives the rules for producing sentences in the language of the system. Systems are themselves objects.

The process of system analysis is to identify the actions and objects and their interaction.
What are the actions?
What are the objects?
What is their program?

The process of system synthesis is to define actions, objects and their interactions.
S = {actions, objects}
actions = {these actions}
objects = {these objects}
program of S = {code list}

The relation of objects and actions is, generally:
S = F(f[t](object[t])) ;where F is a Hal tree.

I will make a series of systems both as an example of system synthesis and as an example of the growth of mathematics from essentials to HalStreams.

The first system to make is the microcontroller (MC) as a mathematical object.

```
MC = {port, ram, code}
 port = {L, R, Out}
 ram = {L, R, M, Out}
 Code = {labels, statements, comments}
labels = {Yes, No, Done, Loop}
statements = {Read,Write,GOTO,IF,=,+,-,*,/}
comments = {anything after ;}
```

All code from here on uses these definitions for code.
For clarity, sometimes I add BEGIN and END statements to set code off from text.

2. A Count system

This is a basic arithmetic system. It has one operation and one object. (The counting numbers.)

AS = {count, N}
count is this following action:

```
BEGIN Count
 N = 0          ;before counting, clear the
count
Loop
 Read I         ;from a constant node
 N = N + I      ;Compute N + I and store it
back to N
 Out = N
 Write Out      ;to another node
 GOTO Loop
END Count
```

Out = Count(I).

Here are some examples of counts by one:
N = i(1)
and
H = 1
He = H + 1
Li = He + 1
Be = Li + 1
B = Be + 1
C = B + 1
N = C + 1
O = N + 1
F = O + 1
Ne = F + 1
and so on for the rest of the elements.

We can define addition of two sets of objects as follows:
Given objects A and objects B, count A and then count B. The count stream will end at A + B.

2. An integer count System

```
IS = {count, uncount, integer}
integer = {-N,0,N}
integer = {... -1,0,1 ...}

Given a set of objects to uncount

BEGIN Uncount
1. uc = Count(s) ; get to starting point
2. Get I
Loop
3. uc = uc - I
4. If no more objects then go to store else go
to loop
Store
5. Send uc to Out
6. Stop
END Uncount
```

Note that uncount requires count.

Subtraction then is:
Given objects A and objects B, count A and uncount B.

uncount requires an integer since it can create negative numbers. The operation is differentiation like. Count and uncount work on one set of objects.

An arithmetic must be defined before we can work on two sets of objects.

{A + B}

An algebra must be defined before we can store the results of the count.

{C = A + B}

2. A Simple Math System

SM = {O, S} ;The system actions and objects.

S = {0,1} ;The objects.

O = {+,-} ;The actions or operations.

If S = 0 Then S + 1 = 1. If S = 1 Then S + 1 = 0.

If S = 0 Then S - 1 = 1. If S = 1 Then S - 1 = 0.

Given two variables of S, namely d1 and d2, we can make an arithmetic and write all the sentences of this system:

d1 + d2 = plus action
d1 - d2 = minus action
(There is no minus sign here so subtraction uses this fact: 0 - 1 is certainly not zero and since we only have 0 and 1 then it must be 1.)

Objects d1	d2	Actions -	+	Comments
0	0	0	0	0 = 0 - 0, 0 = 0 + 0
0	1	1	1	1 = 0 - 1, 1 = 0 + 1
1	0	1	1	1 = 1 - 0, 1 = 1 + 0
1	1	0	0	0 = 1 - 1, 0 = 1 + 1

Note that at this level, we cannot distinguish between operators. Any action, perhaps any possible action, works the same in this system. The system simply does not have the capacity to discriminate between actions. Binary cannot do arithmetic. Binary actions are not the least action you can take. Binary actions are the grossest actions you can do. A Bit selects this half of the universe or that half.

A universal relation between objects and actions is beginning to show itself. The relation is between bit capacity and discrimination. It does not apply just to number codes. A counting system cannot discriminate between addition and multiplication. The square of a counting number can, but not completely. The cube and above of a counting number can discriminate perfectly between addition and multiplication.

2. A Boolean Algebra

The real invention of the computer was in 1938 when Claude Shannon, an employee of Bell Laboratories, wrote a little paper entitled "A Symbolic Analysis of Relay and Switching Circuits". That paper married Boolean algebra to the hardware of switches and relays. The developers of the computer had a means of design, documentation and construction of the computer. This is still in all our integrated circuits. This is what it was. I have added xor.

A simple Boolean algebra is {**and**, **or**, **xor,** **not,** 0,1}
Actions = {**and**, **or,** **xor,** **not**}
Objects = {0,1}
variables {I, L, R, Out}

The programs for the logic operations are:

```
BEGIN and ; Out = L and R
Loop
 Read L
 Read R
 ; Out = L and R
 If L = 1 and R = 1, Out = 1 else Out = 0
 Write Out
 Go to Loop
END and
```

```
BEGIN or  ;    Out = L or R
Loop
 Read L
 Read R
; Out = L or R
 IF L=1 or R=1 or L=R, Out = 1
                         else Out = 0
 Write Out
 GOTO Loop
END or

BEGIN xor ;          Out = I xor R
Loop
 Read L
 Read R
 ; Out = L - R with no borrow
 IF L=0 and R=1 or L=1 and R=0, Out = 1
                    else Out = 0
 Write Out
 GOTO Loop


BEGIN not ;    Out = not(I)
Loop
 Read I
 IF I = 0, Out = 1 else Out = 0
 Write Out
 GOTO Loop
END not
```

Note that these programs do not stop, therefore you can form networks of bit logic and use them to make integrated circuits which are nodes in a bit stream.

Sentence forms are Out = L **and** R, Out = L **or** R,
Out = I **xor** R, and Out = **not**(I). Its sentences are:

L	R			and	xor	or	not(R)	not(L)
0	0			0	0	0	1	1
0	1			0	1	1	0	1
1	0			0	1	1	1	0
1	1			1	0	1	0	0

Not very exciting, is it? Also not complete since only 5 of the 16 logic numbers are used (1, 6, 7 10, 12). All our active machines and computers are built from this algebra. What makes this practical is the program loop adds the time dimension to every variable, creating bit streams.

Let us head on to arithmetic and algebra. This is the foundation for robots.

2. An Integer System

Redo the simple math system by using integers as objects.

SM1 = {-,+, *,integers}

Again, I make a toy system where integers are {-1 to 0 to 1}.

The programs for these, using internal variable names L, R and Out, are:

```
BEGIN Minus
 Read L
 Read R
 Out = L - R
 Stop
END Minus

BEGIN Plus
 Read L
 Read R
 Out = L + R
 Stop
END Plus
```

```
BEGIN Multiply
 M = 0
 Read L
 Read R
 IF L < R, GOTO Yes, GOTO No
Yes
 M = M + R
 L = L - 1
 IF L <= 0, GOTO Done, GOTO Yes
No
 M = M + L
 R = R - 1
 IF R <= 0, GOTO Done, GOTO No
Done
 Out = M
 M = 0
 Write Out
 Stop
END Multiply
```

To complete the arithmetic we sketch an integer divide.
Out = L div R (all positive integers)

```
BEGIN DIV
 Read L
 Read R
 Out = 0
 W = L
 IF L <> 0, GOTO Yes, GOTO Zero
Yes
 IF R <> 0, GOTO Inc, GOTO Zero
Inc
 Out = Out + 1
DoDiv-
 W = W - R
 IF W <= 0, GOTO Fini, GOTO Inc
Zero                   ; is 0 or
 out = 0               ; cannot divide by 0
Fini
 Write Out
 STOP
END DIV
```

We have variables **L**, R and Out for this system. The sentence forms are Out = L - R, Out = L + R, Out = L*R and Out = L/R.

Produce all the sentences of a system by cycling through all the values the variables can take. Start at the lowest value of the variable.

All the sentences for this system are:

I	R	-	+	*	/	
-1	-1	0	-2	1	1	
-1	0	-1	-1	0	-n	n means
-1	1	-2	0	-1	-1	not defined
0	-1	1	-1	0	0	
0	0	0	0	0	-n	
0	1	-1	1	0	0	
1	-1	2	0	-1	-1	
1	0	1	1	0	n	
1	1	0	2	1	1	

Note that, unlike logic, there are patterns that develop here. These patterns persist for all integers. Note the scarcity of the multiplication. With 2 bits, multiplication cannot be distinguished from division and can barely be distinguished from addition and subtraction. With one bit, all arithmetic operations blur together. Only logic is visible.

One more step. We have numbers as integers. An integer stream is a stream of integers such that for any time **t** there is an integer and for any time **t+c** there is another integer. Sensors create integer streams. They provide the input we saw in the logic system. Soon, we will discover general HalStreams.

You can impose an index on an integer stream. An index is an N set beside the integer stream so you can refer to an item in the stream by its ordinal name. For example, here is part of an integer stream:

2,1,3,4,6,2,4,5,9,6,4, 2, 1 ;part of an integer stream

0,1,2,3,4,5,6,7,8,9,10,11,12 ; the index or time.

A notation is needed so we can refer to each item in the integer stream by its index name. First name the integer stream. A = integer stream ; now a simple notation will capture an object in A. Use [ ] as a container for the index number. Then A[1] is first item, A[2] is second item and we can name the index = j and express the general idea A[j] which picks up the jth A. That can also be named so in general one can say B = A[j] which indicates B is one item of the integer stream A.

Note that every integer stream is a replica of our computer memory array. The index is just the address in the computer memory.

2. Integer stream Math

Dss = {-,+, integer streams}

Variables = {I, R, Out}

I repeat the programs for minus and plus with a variation.

```
BEGIN Minus
Loop
 Read L                  ; get L from the outside
 Read R                  ; get R from the outside
 Out = L - R             ; subtract R from L
 Write Out               ; Store Out to the outside
 Go to Loop              ; keep doing this
END Minus

BEGIN Plus
Loop
 Read L                  ; 3
 Read R                  ; 4
 Out = L + R             ; 3+4 = 7
 Write Out
 Go to Loop
END Plus
```

Now, minus and plus never stop, so we can connect them in networks and make universal HalNodes of them. We have added the time dimension to all our variables

A,**B** and **C** are integer stream variables. Sentence forms in this system are **A = B - C** and **A = B + C**. These forms are the same as the static integer form with the addition of direction and implied causality. Most arithmetic still works with this. It is true that if A = B - C that

A = B - C

and B = A + C

and C = A - B, but you need three nodes to express B = A + C and
C = A - B. If you connect all these, of course you will find out that A = A, B = B and C = C.

2. Explicit Functions

A = d(B) says that A is equal to the function d of B. A function has one or more inputs and an output. Here B is an input and A is an output. Functions are little machines that perform an operation on their inputs and send the result to its output.

Functions are actions, with the specific action undefined, that have a single answer. That is, a function is a variable equation.

Here is a program for any single input function

```
Function
BEGIN Function
Loop
 Read I
 Out = f(I)    ;Put an equation here
 Write Out
 GOTO Loop
END Function
```

Note that any and every function reads and writes a data stream.

Integration

```
BEGIN i         Out = i(I)
Out = 0
Loop
 Read I
 Out = Out + I       ; the integration
 Write Out
 GOTO Loop           ; Do this forever
END i
```

Differentiation

```
BEGIN d         Out = d(I)
 M = 0
Loop
 Read I
 Out = I - M         ; Subtract M
 Write Out
 M = I               ; remember I
 GOTO Loop           ; Do this forever
END d
```

Out = L - R I retain for comparing two integer streams. This relationship shows that differentiation and subtraction are the same operation, done in time for **d(B)** and in space for **L - R**. The same applies to **i(B)** and **L + R** for integration. Integration does have, always, a constant of integration attached. This is done with another node, P or C if needed. All HalNodes, HalTrees and neurons are functions. Any operations done on these functions are also functions.

1. Hal Streams

Integer streams can be generalized to HalStreams by loosening the restrictions from integer to more general data. I will next develop a complete Algebra that is to Boolean algebra as arithmetic is to logic.

I impose one restriction here.

I must be able to create hardware for every operator I use.

I impose one requirement here.

Every equation here has connections to every other equation carrying the same variable name. That requires that all actions loop. (A set of equations here is a connected tree network.)

HalStreams represent data moving in time as we will see following.

E -> Sensors -> Brain -> Motors -> E

This shows the general Hal stream flow for any system in an environment. Note that this is a loop or wheel also in that it has feedback through the environment E.

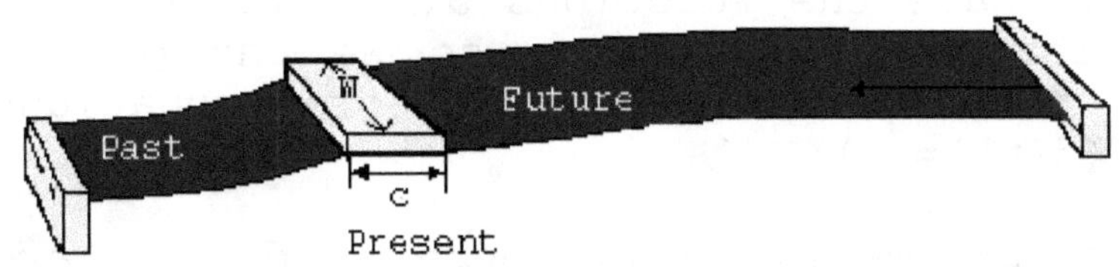

Figure 3 Hal Stream Cable

Hal streams are data moving in time. Hal-Streams carry data from sensors to motors. Every Hal stream variable is two dimensional, the data and the time. Since time is constant, most of the time we can ignore it. (dt = 1). In Cartesian coordinates:

```
     |
     |          all
     |       at      in
Value|   curve            any
     | any                     way
     _________________________________
                Time ->
```

Until HalStreams, all functional curves were static with every point designated with two values. (X, Y). But HalStreams flow, since sensors create each value in time. A necessary property of HalStreams is that there is always a next datum. HalStreams allow calculus to become functional. There is no more dx/dt, instead we have the functions d(x) and i(y) defined for any Hal stream, so we can go directly to differential and integral equations since (d(t) = 1).

HalStreams are everywhere, and they are invisible in the same way that numbers are everywhere and invisible. We need a mechanism to show HalStreams just as we did to show numbers and to show the relationship of numbers to HalStreams.

In the computer we had variables indexed into the memory. Now we use the entire memory as a variable.

Instead of fixed arrays I use ribbon cables with plugs that plug into sensors, motors and nodes. The new variable is now in a cable instead of a box. Sensors emit HalStreams that flow along the cables one value after another.

Now you can label cables with the Hal stream name. You can record samples of HalStreams to contemplate. A Hal stream could be sent to a printer to capture a complete record. Normally you need only representative samples and you can simply write these down on paper. Parts of HalStreams can be graphed on Cartesian coordinates, looking exactly like standard mathematical functions. Parts of HalStreams like this are mathematical sequences and everything known about sequences applies.

Portions of natural number and other HalStreams are sequences. Differentiation corresponds to sequence differences. Some of the work done on sequences is applicable to HalStreams. HalStreams do not end, so we are not interested in computing sums except as we integrate them.

Counting generates polynomial HalStreams. Everything and anything that counts or measures produces a Hal stream. A clock produces a Hal stream of time symbols by counting. The odometer on your car counts miles. A river system counts raindrops. A thermometer measures temperature by counting hits of moving molecules. If you have a calculator with an automatic constant, you can create a Hal stream by entering a number and operation and another number and repeatedly pushing the = key.

In general, we can call anything that converts a measurement to a Hal stream a sensor. Sensors emit HalStreams. The source of every Hal stream is a sensor.

On the other side, anything that converts a Hal stream into a measure is a motor. Motors read HalStreams. The sink of every Hal stream is a motor.

Any sensor can connect to any motor. Motor = Sensor. A node, between motor and sensor is the only place a motor communicates with a sensor. A two input node is one or two motors and one sensor.

Time is associated with every Hal stream. HalStreams add the dimension of time to numbers. There is always the previous number, this number, and the next number cycling through each other. The sensor that creates the Hal stream has a cycle time **c**. Think of the number wheel spinning back and forth. Another Hal stream number follows every other Hal stream number in time **c**. Conventional arithmetic ignores **c**, as in geometry, or implicitly sets it to zero, as in calculus or to 1 as in sequential studies. In nature, there is always a processing time **c**.

If **A** is a Hal stream, you can always reach time in it by indexing it. **A[t-1]** is the previous datum (past). **A[t]** is the present datum and **A[t+1]** is the next datum (future). The sequence is past, present and future. The Hal stream flow is that **A[t-1] = A[t]** and **A[t] = A[t+1]** forever or that future becomes present and recedes to past, a shift every time c. Past is the datum you have finished working with. Present is the datum you are working on. Future is the datum you will be working with next. Integrators and differentiators always use **A[t]** (present) and **A[t-1]** (Past) and thus have memory as a necessary property.

If actual time is required, use **c,** the cycle time, instead of 1. Usually, you do not know the value of **c** and it is better, design wise, to pretend you do not. A system, reading a Hal stream from a sensor has no direct way of knowing whether the sensor is changing the timing of the stream or the data itself is changing. In other words, nature includes the sensors. Brains see sensors, not the world.

Every Hal stream has time in one dimension with its differential on one side and its integral on the other in another dimension.

I have nodes. I have HalStreams. With HalStreams as objects and nodes as actions, I can make an algebra system.

This number system is a single digit, base 256 with the count represented by the decimal symbols from -128 to +127 or the hexadecimal symbols from 80 to 7F or the hexadecimal symbols from 0 to FF or the decimal symbols from 0 to 255. All of these represent the same bit patterns from the digit. Note the sequence, here given in decimal,
-128, -127, -- 0, 1, -- 126,127
like a wheel with 256 symbols painted on it. Imagine that it clicks from symbol to symbol. A click represents a count forward or backward, which represents subtraction and addition. The total number of clicks to recycle is the base. This wheel has 256 clicks.

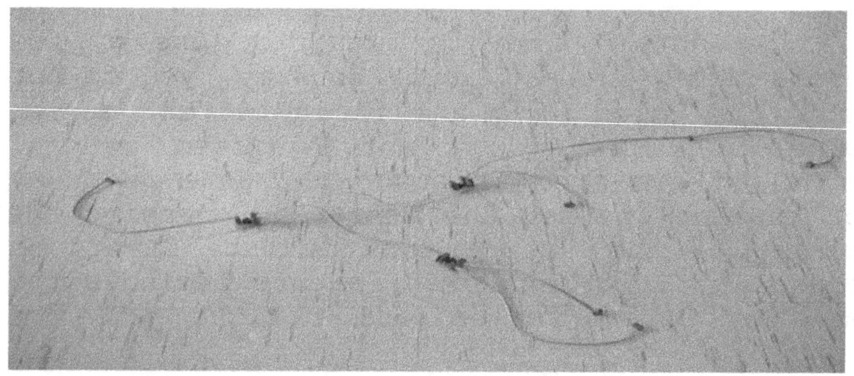

Figure 4 Hal stream Cables & Nodes

2. Hal Algebra

A cable carries a Hal stream, written by a sensor.

A cable can have any number of plugs.

A Hal stream has width (w).

A Hal node is an operator or a function and has a cycle time (c).

Out, I, L, R are headers on Hal nodes and connect Hal stream variables which are plugs on cables.

Out = HalNode or
Out = L HalNode R or
Out = F(HalNode)

The = sign and HalNode are the hardware. Out, I, L and R are headers and are data for the hardware.

HalAlgebra = {sensors, nodes, motors, cables}
nodes = {arithmetic, logic, Switch}
 arithmetic = {tree, single}
  tree = {C, P, O, A, logic}
  single = {I, D, N, B, Not, ABS}
 logic = {GT, LT, IS, WAS, WGT, WLT}
 Switch = {G, L, Z, WG, WG, WL, WZ, DG, DL, DZ, WDG, WDL, WDZ}

-,+, o, a, gt, lt, is, g, l, z, are operators. n, Not, d, i, ABS are functions.
= is transfer operator. (May be read as 'becomes')
; is a comment delimiter.

Here is a table of some HalNodes. All will be described later.

Operator	HalNode	Notation	Description
-	C	O = L - R	Difference
+	P	O = L + R	Sum
Max	o	O = L o R	Max
Min	a	O = L a R	Min
*	MPY	O = L * R	MPY
/	Div	O = L / R	Div
AND	AND	O = L AND R	AND
OR	OR	O = L OR R	OR
XOR	XOR	O = L XOR R	XOR
NOR	NOR	O = L NOR R	NOR Not(or)
i	i	O = i(I)	Integral
d	d	O = d(I)	Derivative

These are the base nodes. As we move toward language semantics, we will need to create more nodes for special projects. Larger constructs, like agents, can be created as needed. The Logic HalNodes, above, were created to add pain to a Robot, to prevent it from hurting itself. This is universal enough to promote it to the basic HalNode list. The ZNode emits R when it detects zero at I. R can be a code or another Hal stream. It is useful for object detection and sequential actions that must wait on each other. It should be noted that a HalNode can be any O = f(I) or O = w(I,R) that you can program in a computer as long as they can read and write HalStreams. If neurons do not do any of these, they are missing the obvious.

In a HalNode - cable system like X = Z - Y, as X becomes Z - Y, complexity is reduced and dimension is reduced. If Z and Y are ramps (complexity[1]), then X is a constant (complexity[0]). X is a point. Z and Y are a line.

Hal stream variables can be integers of any size. If they are reduced to 1 bit, then Boolean arithmetic applies. I make a truth table for 1 bit Nodes. The Hal stream is either 0 or 1. The sequence is 0, 1, 0, 1, 0, 1, 0 … You might note that if this sequence is taken whole, that is as the binary number one oh, one oh, one oh, it becomes the decimal number 42, which is the computer's answer to "Life, the Universe and all" in <u>The Hitchhikers Guide to the Galaxy</u>, a Science fiction satire. In the run of the story, this involves a young Englishman who is trying to block a bulldozer from tearing down his house. He is saved by a guy named Ford Prefect, an alien, who happens to be collecting data for the "Hitchhikers Guide to the Galaxy". Earth also is in the path of a bulldozer. All though the journey our hero is still in his bathrobe. Anyhow, there is this huge computer, somewhere in the galaxy, occupying an entire planet. It is very smart. So it was asked to compute the answer to "life, the universe and all that". What is it? Well the computer took the problem and computed on it for several million years and finally came up with the answer. The galaxy waited anxiously, expecting something grand. The operator walks up to the machine to collect the answer. He gets it, turns and announces it. The answer is: 42.

To show the essence of the basic HalNodes here, we can reduce the Hal stream width to 1 bit, and examine the consequences.

1 bit HalStreams in HalNodes

L	R	C	P	O	A
0	0	0	0	0	0
0	1	1	1	0	1
1	0	1	1	1	0
1	1	0	0	0	0

Note that a C Node is an exclusive or (XOR) unit.
P Node is also an XOR at this bit level.

If the Hal stream integer size is 2 bits, then we have integers of -1, 0, 1. Or in binary twos complement:

Binary Decimal
11 -1
00 0
01 1

This number system sequence is:
-1, 0, 1, -1, 0, 1… ------- 2's complement
3, 0, 1, 3, 0, 1… ------- binary count
11,00,01, 11,00,01… ------- binary code

The truth table for this system is:

2 bit HalStreams

-1 0 1 ; integer

L	R	C	P	O	A
11	11	00	10	11	11
11	00	11	11	11	00
11	01	10	00	11	01
00	11	01	11	11	01
00	00	00	00	00	00
00	01	11	10	01	00
01	11	10	10	11	01
01	00	01	01	01	00
01	01	00	10	10	00

The arithmetic operators come in two classes. The binary operators work on two Hal-Streams. The functions, BNodes, and NNodes work on single HalStreams.

Out = d(I) ; Out = I(Past) - I(Present)
Out = i(I) ; Out = Out(Past) + I
Out = n(I) ; for N nodes
Out = b(I) ; for B nodes
Out = Not(I) ; for Not nodes
Out = ABS(I) ; for ABS nodes

I can show tree nodes as phase space. I list one input variable on one axis and the other input variable on the other axis. The answer to any values of the two variables is found by finding the intersection of the two lines drawn from the variables.

Out = L - R

```
          C node
   .
   .
   3 |  3  2  1  0
L  2 |  2  1  0 -1
   1 |  1  0 -1 -2
   0 |  0 -1 -2 -3
        ----------
        0  1  2  3 . . .
              R
```

Here is a quick proof that comparison and differentiation is the same thing.

Out = I[2] - I[1]

```
            D node
     .
     .
     3 |  3  2  1  0
I[2] 2 |  2  1  0 -1
     1 |  1  0 -1 -2
     0 |  0 -1 -2 -3
          ----------
          0  1  2  3 . . .
              I[1]
```

This results in the same phase space with a simple change of variable names.
Proof is done.

The corollary of this is that every two input difference equation differentiates. Out **= L - R**. Out is the change of **L** related to **R**.

The same thing applies to integration and addition for one datum only. P nodes have no memory. I nodes remember count.

P node

Out = L + R

```
        .
        3 | 3  4  5  6
L       2 | 2  3  4  5
        1 | 1  2  3  4
        0 | 0  1  2  3
            ----------
            0  1  2  3 …
                 R
```

I node

Out = I[1] + I[2]

```
       .
       3 | 3  4  5  6
I[1]   2 | 2  3  4  5
       1 | 1  2  3  4
       0 | 0  1  2  3
           ----------
           0  1  2  3 …
                I[2]
```

Again, a simple change of variable names gives the proof.

Now look at the behavior of the GT Node.

GT node

Out = L gt R ;
Out = L-R if L > R else Out = 0

L		0	1	2	3	4 …
	4	0	3	2	1	0
	3	0	2	1	0	0
L	2	0	1	0	0	0
	1	0	0	0	0	0
	0	0	0	0	0	0

R

LT node

Out = L lt R ;
Out = L-R if L < R else Out = 0

L		0	1	2	3	4 …
	4	0	0	0	0	0
	3	0	0	0	0	-1
L	2	0	0	0	-1	-2
	1	0	0	-1	-2	-3
	0	0	-1	-2	-3	-4

R

IS node

Out = L is R ;
Out = L if L = R else Out = 0

L		0	1	2	3	4 …
	4	0	0	0	0	4
	3	0	0	0	3	0
	2	0	0	2	0	0
	1	0	1	0	0	0
	0	1	0	0	0	0

R

G node

Out = L G R ;
Out = R if L > 0 else Out = 0

L		0	1	2	3	4 …
	4	0	1	2	3	4
	3	0	1	2	3	4
	2	0	1	2	3	4
	1	0	1	2	3	4
	0	0	0	0	0	0 …

R

L node

Out = L l R;

Out = R if L < 0 else Out = 0

```
          .
          4 |  0   0   0   0   0
          3 |  0   0   0   0   0
    L     2 |  0   0   0   0   0
          1 |  0   0   0   0   0
          0 |  0   0   0   0   0
         -1 |  0   1   2   3   4
               -----------------
               0   1   2   3   4 …
                       R
```

Z node

Out = L z 0 ;

Out = R if L = 0 else Out = 0

```
          .
          4 |  0   0   0   0   0
          3 |  0   0   0   0   0
    L     2 |  0   0   0   0   0
          1 |  0   0   0   0   0
          0 |  0   1   2   3   4 …
               --------------------
               0   1   2   3   4 …
                       R
```

2. Analog Sensors

The front end of every sensor is usually an analog device. Use the relation

V = I*R.

The sensor can be a variable resister (R) or a variable current (I). Provide a positive current source V+. Current flows through R to ground (G) producing a voltage (V) that is from 0 to V+, always positive, representing the value of the thing you are sensing. This voltage can be fed into an analog to digital converter (ADC) directly to give us a number Hal stream. If the sensor goes both positive and negative, then you need to convert to all positive before going digital. Some ADCs do not know about negative voltages.

2. HalNode Hardware Interface Specifications

This specification is addressed to those who build sensors of all kinds to sense the outside world and those who build actuators, motors and so on to act on the outside world.

Hal stream Cables

HalStreams are carried physically on standard 4 wire flat cable. 4 pin IDC sockets are positioned on the cable where required. These plug into 4 pin headers on the HalNodes or on your nodes.

Pinouts
Cable, Sockets and Headers

Pin	Name	Function	Header
1	Power3 to 6 volts		1 2
2	Ground	system ground	3 4
3	IC, OC	clock	
4	ID, OD	data	

Pin 1 orientation should be observed but boards will not be zapped if cables are reversed. (Power is provided by 4 NiMH batteries.) Power supplies should have one 4 pin header with all data lines not connected. Every separate HalTree can have its own power supply.

We still have to work from volts to numbers and number to volts. So there is an analog connection. This uses exactly the same four wire cable and connectors. All sensors and motors have 4 pin headers. All ADC and MoNodes have one 4 pin header. The system, analog sensor, ADC is the sensor in Hal algebra. The system MoNode, motor, gearbox is a motor in Hal algebra.

Analog Connectors

Pin	Name	Function	Header
1	Power	5 volts	1 2
2	Ground	ground	3 4
3	Util	NC or data	
4	data	data	

Now we can go inside some representative HalNodes and see the elementary things they do. We will become each node, starting at the beginning. This is back to neuron functions as I have developed them over the years. Here they are presented in all detail with all the PIC code and platform required to produce them.

1. Inside HalNodes

2. Sensors

2. Creating HalStreams - Sensors

Nature -> **Sensors** -> Brain -> Motors -> Nature

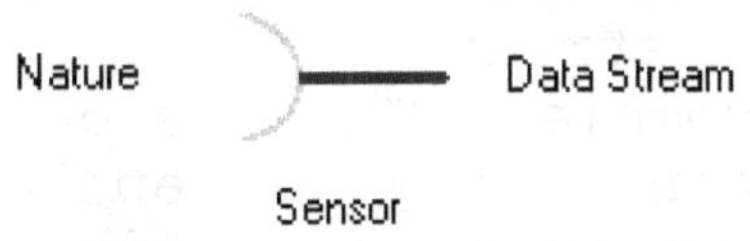

Nature Data Stream

Sensor

Out = f(Nature)

You are a sensor. The job of a sensor is to create and write a Hal stream from nature. Sensors decode and abstract from nature. As a sensor, you sit half in nature and half in a brain, at the limits of the body. You the sensor, sense one item from nature. You are the fetch machine for this Hal stream. Your output is the axon if you are a neuron.

You have a window to some feature of nature. You have a calculator. (All Hal stream manipulators have calculators and data storage registers if needed. Hal stream creators and consumers have all the tools of technical history available as required.)

The operation of a sensor is:

1. Observe the sensor quantity through the window.
2. Compute the number **O(t)**. Make it an integer.
3. Write the number to Out
4. Go to 1. ; Cycle time is Cs.

Operation 1 observes nature. The means of observation can be electromagnetic, pressure, heat or inertial (light, sound, temperature or acceleration). Every HalNode is a virtual sensor since it creates a Hal stream.

Operation 2 can be complex. This is generally the process of converting an analog quantity into a number, as fast as possible. Sensors can be classified as to type and can be made universal with integer output. Then you can buy them off the shelf. The numbers produced by us as a sensor may be integers but you should not do anything else to them. No integration or differentiation should be done. Sensors have no memory. Sensors sit half in the world and half in the brain. In various applications, sensors encode and abstract from nature to some data type.

It takes a time, c, to create the sensor Hal stream. Data can arrive in nanoseconds, microseconds, milliseconds, seconds, minutes, hours, days, months and years. To make any Hal stream differentiable you follow the rule of keeping a datum available until there is a new datum, regardless of the interval between them. This makes the Hal stream solid, with no intervals of bad data. If the data is faster than you can pick it up then you will skip some data and the output Hal stream will be a sample of the incoming data. If the data is very slow, then there might be intervals of constant data.

The sensor adds time to the sensed variable. The output Hal stream is two dimensional, time is added to the data stream and time is always implied in every Hal stream variable.

The HalStreams emitted by a sensor can be of any type.

k	constant
kN	Line of slope k
Nx	Combinatorial numbers of degree x
kPx	All polynomials of scale k and degree x
f(x,t)	Any function of a variable

In practice, you must be careful to note the type of output you provide from the sensor. In the analog world, differentiation and integration can occur by accident. Generally, a series capacitor will differentiate. A parallel capacitor will integrate. Your specifications should specify if you do either.

Some sensor types are:
1. Temperature
2. Pressure
3. Light
4. Acceleration
5. Time
6. Numeric pad
7. Latitude and longitude
8. Radio
9. GPS

Units are those of length, mass, time, electric current, temperature and luminous intensity. Sensors should always be used in pairs. With pairs of sensors, you control another parameter.

A single sensor "sees" a single spot. A pair of sensors "sees" a single object. The distance between the sensors determines the minimum size of the object that can be detected. Increasing the distance increases the area covered and decreases discrimination. However, using another pair of sensors at a greater distance like this also increases the area covered while preserving size:

S1-S2---------------S3-S4 ; general
LL-LR---------------RL-RR ; left and right

There are nodes between sensors and other nodes, to convert units into numbers. The most general of these is the ADCNode, which converts voltage into number. There is also an RCNode which converts a radio control servo signal into an integer. Other types can be developed as needed.

The sensor part that looks at nature has a field of view. You measure field of view as a solid angle. A field of view can be represented by a cone radiating from the sensor. Everything inside the cone is on and everything outside is invisible or off. The angle of the cone can go from zero, completely closed to 180 degrees. (You can rotate to get the full 360 degrees, since it is symmetric.) You, the sensor have to be held by the body or body part. This by itself determines some of the field of view. Quite often you have to manipulate the field of view with a lens. Mainly you want to make it easy for the brain to see out there instead of in here.

What makes this important is that with multiple sensors, the fields overlap and form a pattern in space. This encodes a lot of information for the brain.

Mechanically, I have these sensor nodes:
1. NbrNode puts a constant on the data cable. At present it is 8 switches, which means it can be used for general switch detection.

All circuit boards are approximately actual size.

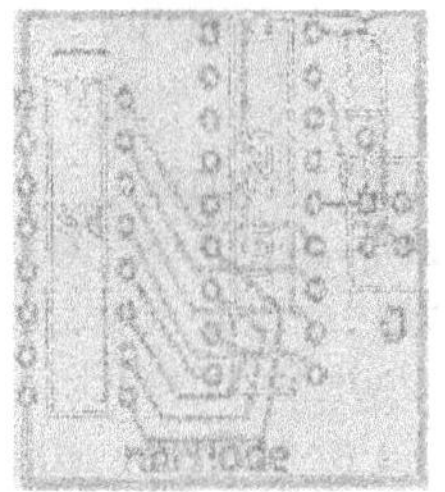

Figure 5 NbrNode

Here is the code for NbrNode:

```
; PIC16F627 program for nbrNode Revision 1
; use FOSC2:FOSC0 bits 100 = INTRC osc: I/O function on
RA6,RA7
; disable low voltage programming
; All pins except power and ground are I/O.
; SOut = I
; This routine can be used for any switch input func-
tion source
 LIST p=16F627, w=1
;       Constants
Reads         EQU  0FFh  ;All bits read
Writes        EQU  00h   ;All bits write
; Port and header pins
OC            EQU   01h   ;PortA,1 to O header 3
OD            EQU   00h   ;PortA,0 to O header 4
;
; Registers
STATUS        EQU   03h   ;status register
T1CON         EQU   10h   ;Timer1 control(disable)
CMCOM         EQU   01Fh  ;Comparator control
; Bank 1 registers
OPTIONR       EQU   81h
TRISA         EQU   85h   ;PortA tristate
TRISB         EQU   86h   ;PortB
PIE1          EQU   8Ch   ;Interrupt control
;
;      Ports
PortA         EQU   05h   ;output
PortB         EQU   06h   ;input
;      Variables
I             EQU   020h
Out           EQU   021h
D             EQU   022h
TT            EQU   023h
;
;
 ORG          0
 BCF          T1CON,3     ;disable t1 osc
 CLRF PortA
 MOVLW        07h
 MOVWF        CMCOM       ;turn off comparators
;
```

```
 BSF         STATUS,5    ;bank 1
 BCF         TRISA,0     ;set PortA for output
 BCF         TRISA,1     ;bits 0,1 output
 CLRF PIE1         ;turn off interrupts
 CLRF OPTIONR      ;turn on weak pullups
 MOVLW       Reads
 MOVWF       TRISB       ;set up input
 BCF         STATUS,5    ;Bank 0
 BCF         PortA,OC
 BCF         PortA,OD
;
Loop
 CLRWDT                  ;WDT = 0
; read I
 MOVF        PortB,W     ; W = PortB
 MOVWF       I           ; I = W
;
; Begin NbrNode function
;
 COMF I,1          ;1 I = Not(I)
 MOVF I,W          ;2 W = I
 MOVWF       Out         ;3 Out = W
;
; end NbrNode function
;
; Do Output
;
; make start time
 MOVLW       014h        ; W = 14h
 MOVWF       TT          ; TT = W
DTime
 NOP                     ; W = W
 NOP                     ; W = W
 DECFSZ      TT          ; TT = TT - 1
 GOTO DTime        ; [no] (time = 5*TT )
 CLRF D            ; [yes] D = 0
WriteO
 BCF         PortA,OC    ; OC = 0
 NOP                     ;
 BCF         PortA,OD    ; OD = 0
;
```

```
 BTFSS      Out,0       ; Out[0] = 1 ?
 GOTO ZeroO       ; [no]
 BSF        PortA,OD    ; [yes] OD = 1
 GOTO ComO        ;
ZeroO
 BCF        PortA,OD    ; OD = 0
 NOP                    ; W = W
ComO
 BSF        PortA,OC    ; OC = 1
 NOP                    ; W = W
 NOP                    ; W = W
 BCF        STATUS,0    ; STATUS[0] = 0
 RRF        Out,1       ; Out[j] = Out[j+1]
 INCF D           ; D = D + 1
 BTFSS      D,3         ; is D[3] on?
 GOTO       WriteO      ; [no]
;
 BCF        PortA,OC    ; [yes] OC = 0
 BCF        PortA,OD    ; OD = 0
;--------------------------------------------------
;
 GOTO       Loop        ;
;
; end Node
 END Nbr
```

2. ADCNode converts a voltage to an integer.

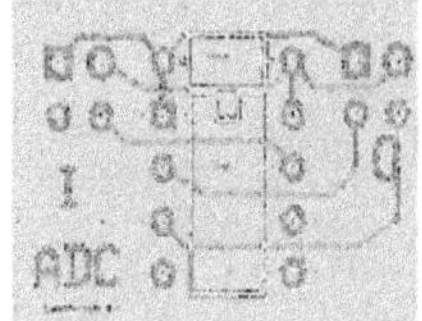

Figure 6 ADCNode

Here is the code for ADCNode:

```
; PIC12F675 program for ADC
; Out = AD of I, 0 to 255 to -128 to 127
; Use internal ADC.
; Begin ADCNode
 LIST p=PIC12F675, w=1
; Constants
; Node constants
Int          EQU   80h   ;integer conversion
;
OC           EQU   05h   ;O output control
OD           EQU   04h   ;Output data
IA           EQU   00h   ;analog in
;
; Bank 0
STATUS       EQU   03h
GPIO         EQU   05h
INTCON       EQU   0Bh
PIR1         EQU   0Ch
TICON EQU    10h
CMCON EQU    19h
ADRESH       EQU   1Eh
ADCON0       EQU   1Fh
;
; Bank 1
OPTIONR      EQU   81h
TRISR EQU    85h
PIE1         EQU   8Ch
PCON         EQU   8Eh
OSCCAL       EQU   90h
WPU          EQU   95h
IOC          EQU   96h
VRCON EQU    99h
EEDATA       EQU   9Ah
EEADR EQU    9Bh
EECON1       EQU   9Ch
EECON2       EQU   9Dh
ADRESL       EQU   9Eh
ANSEL EQU    9Fh
;
```

```
;     Variables
Out         EQU   020h
temp        EQU   021h
Count EQU   022h
TT          EQU   023h
D           EQU   024h
;
 ORG        00h
 BSF        STATUS,5     ;bank1
 CALL 3FFh        ;get calibration
 MOVWF      OSCCAL       ; OSCCAL = W
; do bank1 init
 CLRF       OPTIONR      ;option
 CLRF       PIE1         ; PIE1 = 0
 CLRF       PCON         ; PCON = 0
 CLRF       WPU          ; WPU = 0
 CLRF       IOC          ; IOC = 0
 CLRF       VRCON        ; VRCON = 0
 CLRF       ANSEL        ; ANSEL = 0
; set up Port
 BSF        TRISR,IA     ; P0 is an input
 BSF        TRISR,1      ; P1 is an input
 BCF        TRISR,2      ; P2 dig output
 BSF        TRISR,3      ; P3 dig input
 BCF        TRISR,OD     ; OD P4 data out
 BCF        TRISR,OC     ; OC P5 control out
;
 BCF        STATUS,5     ; STATUS[5] = 0 (bank0)
 CLRF PIR1         ; PIR1 = 0
 CLRF TICON        ; TICON = 0
 CLRF CMCON        ; CMCON = 0
 CLRF ADCON0       ; ADCON0 = 0 (Sets left just)
 BSF        ADCON0,0     ; ADCON0[0] = 1 (turn on ADC)
;
```

```
Loop
 CLRWDT
;
; Begin ADCNode function
;
 BCF         PIR1,6       ; PIR1[6] = 0 (clear ADIF)
 BSF         ADCON0,1     ; ADCON0[1] = 1 (Go/Done=1)
L1
 BTFSS       PIR1,6       ; PIR1[6] = 1 ?
 GOTO        L1           ; [no], go wait
 MOVF        ADRESH,W     ; [yes], W = ADRESH Value
 MOVWF       Out          ; Out = W
 MOVLW       Int          ; W = 80h
 SUBWF       Out,1        ; Out = Out - W makes Out an
integer
;
; End ADCNode function
;-----------------------------------------
 MOVLW       014h         ; W = 14h (make start time)
 MOVWF       TT           ; TT = W
DTime
 NOP                      ; W = W
 NOP                      ; W = W
 DECFSZ      TT           ; TT = TT - 1, is TT=0 ?
 GOTO DTime         ; [no]
 CLRF D             ; [yes] D = 0
WriteO
 BCF  GPIO,OC       ; OC = 0 (set control off)
 BCF  GPIO,OD       ; OD = 0 (set data off)
; write bit
 BTFSS       Out,0        ; Out[0] = 1 ? (test bit of
Out)
 GOTO        ZeroO        ; [no]
 BSF  GPIO,OD       ; [yes] OD = 1 (send one)
 GOTO        ComO         ;
ZeroO
 BCF  GPIO,OD       ; OD = 0 (send zero)
 NOP
```

```
                    ; W = W
; bit written
ComO
 BSF  GPIO,OC     ; OC = 0 (set control on)
 NOP                    ; W = W
 NOP                    ; W = W
 BCF  STATUS,0    ; STATUS[0] = 0
 RRF  Out,1       ; Out[j] = Out[j+1]
 INCF       D           ; D = D + 1
 BTFSS      D,3         ; d[3] = 1 ? (test count)
 GOTO       WriteO      ; [no] (continue if count done)
;
 BCF  GPIO,OC     ; OC = 0 (set control off)
 BCF  GPIO,OD     ; OD = 0 (set data off between words)
;--------------------------------------------------
;
 GOTO       Loop
; end ADCNode
 END
```

2. Brain

Sensors feed data to the brain. All the nodes that follow, until we get to motors, belong to brain. There are two brain node platforms. TNodes have one input and one output. SNodes have two inputs and one output. TNodes make functions of a single Hal stream. SNodes make function trees.

3. TNodes

We start with the single input, single output nodes. These are TNodes and are the hardware platform for TNodes, MoNodes, SMNodes. Here is a picture of the circuit board:

Figure 7 TNodes

Keep this in mind for the descriptions and code that follows.

All TNodes Read I, Do function, Write O. Only functions differ for each node. Required is:

```
Prefix for node.
 [INIT] PIC initiation code
Loop
 [READ I]
 Do function
 [WRITE O]
 GOTO Loop
 END
```

For reference here is [INIT]

```
; Setup for 12F629 TNodes
;
 LIST p=12F629, w=1
; Constants
; Node constants
IC    EQU   05h   ;I control input pin
ID    EQU   04h   ;I data input pin
;
RC    EQU   03h   ;R control input pin
RD    EQU   02h   ;R data input pin
;
OC    EQU   01h   ;O Output control pin
OD    EQU   00h   ;O output data pin
;
; Bank 0 registers
STATUS      EQU   03h
GPIO        EQU   05h   ;I/O port
INTCON      EQU   0Bh
PIR1        EQU   0Ch
TICON       EQU   10h
CMCON       EQU   19h
ADRESH      EQU   1Eh
ADCON       EQU   1Fh
;
```

```
; Bank 1 registers
OPTIONR        EQU   81h
TRISIO         EQU   85h
PIE1           EQU   8Ch
PCON           EQU   8Eh
OSCCAL         EQU   90h
WPU            EQU   95h
IOC            EQU   96h
VRCON          EQU   99h
EEDATA         EQU   9Ah
EEADR          EQU   9Bh
EECON1         EQU   9Ch
EECON2         EQU   9Dh
ADRESL         EQU   9Eh
ANSEL          EQU   9Fh
;
; General variables
L      EQU   20h   ; Left input
R      EQU   21h   ; Right input
Out    EQU   22h   ; Output
D      EQU   23h   ; IO count
TT     EQU   24h   ; temporary count variable
DI     EQU   25h   ; Intermediate variable
M      EQU   26h   ; memory variable
;
 ORG          00h
 BCF          STATUS,5     ; STATUS[5] = 0 (bank0)
 CLRF         GPIO         ; GPIO = 0
 MOVLW        07h          ; W = 07h
 MOVWF        CMCON ; CMCON = W (comparator off)
 CLRF         PIR1         ; PIR1 = 0
 CLRF         TICON        ; TICON = 0
;
 BSF          STATUS,5     ; STATUS[5] = 1 (bank1)
 CALL         3FFh         ; get calibration
 MOVWF        OSCCAL       ; OSCCAL = W (set it)
; do bank1 init
 CLRF         OPTIONR      ; OPTIONR = 0 (option)
 CLRF         PIE1         ; PIE1 = 0
 CLRF         PCON         ; PCON = 0
 CLRF         WPU          ;  WPU  =  0  (Disable  weak
pullups)
 CLRF         IOC          ; IOC = 0 (disable
```

```
                              ;interrupt on change)
 CLRF         VRCON           ; VRCON = 0
; set IO
 MOVLW        3Ch             ;W = 3Ch(5,4,3,2 in 1,0
                        ;out)
 MOVWF        TRISIO          ; TRISIO = W
;
 BCF          STATUS,5        ; STATUS[5] = 0 (bank 0)
 CLRF         GPIO            ; GPIO = 0
;
```

Loop

[READ I]

```
;------------------------------------------
ReadI
;Find start
 MOVLW        04h             ; W = 04h (4, 9, 18)
 MOVWF        TT              ; TT = W (bit, halfword,
                        ;whole word)
CI
 BTFSC        GPIO,IC         ; IC = 0 ? (look at IC)
 GOTO         ReadI           ; [no] is on
 DECFSZ       TT              ; TT = TT - 1
 GOTO         CI              ; [no] 5*TT
; found start, read the word.
 CLRF         D               ; [yes] D = 0 (start with bit
0)
 CLRF         TT              ; TT = 0
 BCF          STATUS,0        ; STATUS[0] = 0
I1
 BTFSC        GPIO,IC         ; IC = 0? (bit Low?)
 GOTO         RDIBit          ; [no] is high, go read
 DECFSZ       TT              ; [yes], TT = TT - 1 (time it)
 GOTO         I1              ; [no] try again
 GOTO         GotI            ; [yes] give up
; read bit
RDIBit
 BTFSS        GPIO,ID         ; ID = 1? test bit
 GOTO         ZeroI           ; [no] is zero
 BSF          I,7             ; [yes] I[7] = 1 (is one,
                        ; move it to I)
 GOTO         ComI            ;
```

```
ZeroI
 BCF        I,7           ; I[7] = 0 (move bit to I)
 NOP                      ; W = W
; bit read.
ComI
 INCF       D             ; D = D + 1 next bit
 BTFSC      D,3           ; d[3] = 1 ? (bits done?)
 GOTO       GotI          ; [no]
 BCF        STATUS,0      ; [yes] STATUS[0] = 0
 RRF        I,1           ; I[j] = I[j+1]
 GOTO       I1            ; (Do until bits are done)
GotI

;---------------------------------------------------
 DO TNode function
[WRITE Out]
;----------------------------------------
 MOVLW      014h          ; W = 14h (make start time)
 MOVWF      TT            ; TT = W
DTime
 NOP                      ; W = W
 NOP                      ; W = W
 DECFSZ     TT            ; TT = TT - 1, is it 0?
 GOTO       DTime         ; [no]
 CLRF       D             ; [yes] D = 0
WriteO
 BCF        GPIO,OC       ; OC = 0 (set control off)
 BCF        GPIO,OD       ; OD = 0 (set data off)
; write bit
 BTFSS      Out,0         ; Out[0] = 1? (test bit of Out)
 GOTO       ZeroO         ;
 BSF        GPIO,OD       ; OD = 1 (send one)
 GOTO       ComO          ;
ZeroO
 BCF        GPIO,OD       ; OD = 0 (send zero)
 NOP                      ; W = W
; bit written
ComO
 BSF        GPIO,OC       ; OC = 1 (set control on)
 NOP                      ; W = W
 NOP                      ; W = W
 BCF        STATUS,0      ; STATUS[0] = 0
 RRF        Out,1         ; Out[j] = Out[j+1]
```

```
 INCF       D            ; D = D + 1
 BTFSS      D,3          ; D[3] = 1? (test count)
 GOTO       WriteO       ;  [no]  (or  continue  if  count
done)
;
 BCF        GPIO,OC      ; OC = 0 (set control off)
 BCF        GPIO,OD      ; OD = 0 (set data off between
words)
;--------------------------------------------------
 GOTO Loop
 END
```

4. Offsetting HalStreams - B Node

Nature -> Sensors -> **Brain** -> Motors -> Nature

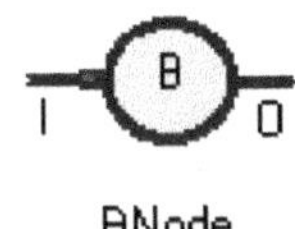

BNode

We start the brain with the smallest and simplest of HalNodes. In the brain you are both motor and sensor. You read and write. You have synapse and axon. You do not change dimension of the Hal stream.

Here you are a BNode. Your job is to catch the input and add 128 to the eight bit input number. This is enough to convert -127 to 128 to 0 to 255 and backward, just like magic since we roll the base 256 wheel over each time. Since the HalNode is working in binary, the numbers (in hexadecimal) show how it works:

O	Offset to integer	I	Integer to offset
00	80	00	80
01	81	01	81
...	...	...	...
...	...	...	...
80	00	80	00
81	01	81	01
...	...	...	...
...	...	...	...
FF	7F	FF	7F

Since we are working on a single Hal stream it is easier to express this HalNode as a function.

The HalNode equation is:
O = b(I)
The BNode program is very simple:
BNode
1. Read I
2. Add 128
3. Write to O
4. Go to 1.

Here is the BNode code:

```
; program for Bnode
; Out = I + 80h
 [INIT]
Loop
 [READ I]
;--------------------------------------------------
;
; Begin BNode function
;
 MOVLW   H'080'            ; W = 80h
 ADDWF   I,0               ; W = W + I
 MOVWF   Out               ; Out = W
;
; end BNode function
;
; Do Output
;----------------------------------------------
 [WRITE O]
 GOTO        Loop
; end Node
 END
```

This HalNode is used when your sensor is providing numbers from 0 to 255, all positive, and you must make an integer right away. Since a CNode always creates integers, this HalNode is seldom needed. If you have a dumb DAC then a BNode will assure it gets values from 0 to 256 as the DAC expects.

4. Negating HalStreams --- N Node

Nature -> Sensors -> **Brain** -> Motors -> Nature

NNode

O = N(I)

Another simple HalNode. You are an NNode. Your job is to take each input number and subtract it from 0. Like the BNode above, the negation works both ways. Again since we are working on a single Hal stream we use a functional notation. The NNode equation is:

O = n(I) or **O = -I** where there is no possible confusion.

The NNode program is:
NNode
1. Read I
2. Subtract from 0
3. Write to O
4. Go to 1.

Here is the NNode code:

```
; program for NNodes
; Out = 0 - I
 [INIT]
Loop
 [READ I]
;-----------------------------------------------------
; Begin N function
 CLRF       DI          ; DI = 0
 MOVF       I,W         ; W = I
 SUBWF      DI,0        ; W = DI - I
 MOVWF      Out         ; Out = W
; End N function
; Do Output
 [WRITE O]
 GOTO       Loop        ;
;
; end NNode
 END
```

4. A Function HalNode ---- Not Node

Nature -> Sensors -> **Brain** -> Motors -> Nature

NotNode

Out = Not(I)

You are a NotNode. Your job is to make binary logical reversals of meaning. You are a function that observes I. If I is zero, you send out 1, else you send out zero. A Not node is used to complete all the conditional Hal-Nodes. Put it in front of a Z node and you have a not Z and so on. It is binary logical because it cares not for values except one and zero.

0. Make OldI
1. Observe the I Hal stream
2. If the I datum is zero, set out = OldI else set out = 0
3. Write out
4. go to 1.

As assembler code:

```
NotNode
 OldI = 3
Loop
 Read I
 If I = 0 then OldI = I and O = OldI else O =
0
 Write O
 Go To Loop
```

As spreadsheet function. A2 is input.
=if(A2=0,A1,0) ;cannot do OldI here.

This is not like the spread sheet NOT function, since the spread sheet returns True and False. Of course True is one and False is zero. This is not a Boolean NOT, it is an arithmetical Not.

NotNode truth table

O = Not(I)

I	O
-1	0
-1	0
-1	0
0	-1
0	-1
0	-1
1	0
1	0
1	0

Here is the code for NotNode:

```
; Program for NotNodes
; Out = Not I
; Begin NotNode
 [INIT]
 MOVLW       03h            ; W = 3
 MOVWF       M              ; M = W
Loop
 [READ I]
;------------------------------------------------------
;
; Begin Not function
;
 MOVF        I,W            ; W = I
 BTFSS       STATUS,2       ; Is W = 0?
 GOTO        NotZ           ; [no]
 MOVF        M,W            ; [yes], W = M
 GOTO        Fini           ;
NotZ
 MOVF        I,W            ; W = I
 MOVWF       M              ; M = W
 CLRW                       ; W = 0
Fini
 MOVWF       Out            ; Out = W
;
; End Not function
;
 [WRITE O]
 GOTO    Loop
;
; end NotNode
 END
```

Note: M is used so we have a little bit of memory. This provides some redundancy for the Robot. If the input is always 0, then Not node defaults to 3.

4. A Function HalNode ---- ABS

Nature -> Sensors -> **Brain** -> Motors -> Nature

ABS Node

Out = ABS(I)

You are an absolute function. Sometimes we are not interested in direction, only in magnitude. You determine the sign on the I input and make Out positive.

```
ABS
 Read I
 If I < 0 then send complement of I to O else
O = I
 Write O
 GOTO ABS
```

Suppose you have rudder and propeller. You have sensor L and sensor R. rudder = L - R
If we only want to move forward then let
propeller = ABS(rudder)

L	R	rudder	propeller
0	0	0	0
0	1	-1	1
1	0	1	1
1	1	0	0

Here is the ABS code:

```
; Begin ABS
 [INIT]
Loop
 [READ I]
; Begin ABS function
 BTFSS      I,7         ;I < 0?
 GOTO       Pos         ;no, (leave alone)
 COMF       I,1         ;yes, I = Not(I)
 INCF       I,1         ; I = I + 1
Pos
 MOVF       I,W         ; W = I
 MOVWF      Out         ; Out = W
; End ABS function
; Do Output
 [WRITE O]
 GOTO       Loop
; end Node
 END
```

4. Differencing a Hal stream - -- D Node

Nature -> Sensors -> **Brain** -> Motors -> Nature

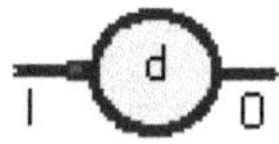

DNode

Out = d(I)

You are a DNode, a single input HalNode.

The job of a differencing function is to subtract each incoming datum from the Hal stream, and send the difference out as a new Hal stream. A curve comes into us and we emit the instructions for making that curve. d(x) = dx/dt because
dt = 1 in every Hal stream. You read I and produce d(I).

O = d(I) ;Example: Acceleration = d(Velocity)

1. Look at the input Hal stream datum **I[j]**.
2. Subtract the memory M.
3. Write **O[j] = I[j] - M**.
4. **M = I[j]**
5. Go to 1. ; Cycle time is Cd.

As assembler code:

```
DNode
Start
 OldIn = 0
Loop
 Read I
 Out = I - OldIn
 Write Out
 OldIn = I
 Go To Loop
End
```

To difference by hand:
Write down the Hal stream sequence like this:

j =	1	2	3	4…
DS =	2	4	6	8…
d(DS) =		2	2	2…

Note: d(DS)[j] = DS[j] - DS[j-1] for every j

O[j] = I[j] - I[j-1] ; j > 0

In a calculator:
1. Enter the jth number. (DS[j])
2. Subtract the j-1th number. (DS[j] - DS[j-1])
3. Record the subtraction.
4. Move to the next number. (j=j+1)
5. Go to 2.

In a spreadsheet you can only difference a column or row. Suppose you have a column of numbers in B. Then d(B) would be the spreadsheet column:
= B2 - B1 ; replicated down its own column.

In truth tables HalStreams are written going down in a column. In the DNode, think of I as a Hal stream, not as a number.

DNode truth table

I	O	
1	x	; I is a triangular wave here.
2	1	
3	1	
2	-1	
1	-1	

To difference, you must also have memory, but only for one past datum. Because the derivative of a constant is zero, a DNode strips off offsets. The derivative of … 25,26… is the same as the derivative of …1,2… To obtain a derivative you must have at least two numbers. The offset that you throw away is the very first number in the Hal stream. Real DNodes produce continuous differences of their input HalStreams and any idea of a first number is lost. Every Hal stream can be differenced as long as there are two numbers available.

In the domain of Hal streams, DNodes obey all the rules of calculus without the restriction of requiring a limiting process.

```
C1 = d(C0)
C2 = d(C1)
C3 = d(C2)
C4 = d(C3)
```

You can also express this as:
k = d5(C0) ; saying k is the 5th derivative of C0
Note that d5(C0) = C4 - 4*C3 + 6*C2 - 4*C1 + C0 and that we need 5 numbers to do that. So dn(x) requires n numbers.

Here is the DNode code:

```
; program for DNodes
; INTRC osc:
; All pins except power and ground are I/O.
; Out = I[j] - I[j+1]
; Begin DNode
 [INIT]
 CLRF       OldI
Loop
 [READ I]
;---------------------------------------------
;
; Begin DNode function
;
 MOVF       OldI,W       ; W = OldI
 SUBWF      I,0          ; W = I - W
 MOVWF      Out          ; Out = W
; Cycle data
 MOVF       I,W          ;4 W = I
 MOVWF      OldI         ;5 OldI = W
;
; End DNode function
;
; Do Output
 [WRITE O]
 GOTO       Loop
;
; end Node
 END
```

A DNode is also a virtual motor and a virtual sensor, so those properties attach to it also.

4. Integrating a Hal stream ----- I Node

Nature -> Sensors -> **Brain** -> Motors -> Nature

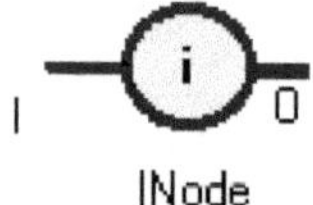

You are an INode. **Out = i(I)**

The incoming Hal stream I is a set of instructions on how to make a curve. The instructions are: go up so much, stay here, or go down so much. The result of this is to build a curve, generally from another curve.

The job of an integrator is to add each incoming datum from the Hal stream to a count, and send the count out as a new Hal stream. Any integration needs a constant simply because the differential of a constant is zero and we obey the rules of calculus. In a Hal stream, additions and subtractions of constants produce a phase shift. To use a constant with an INode, use it outside like Out = i(I) + k

Out = i(I) ; Example : Velocity = i(Acceleration)

i(I)[j] = i(I)[j-1] + I[j]

The operations are:

1. Look at the last Hal stream integral **O[j-1].**
2. Add the input Hal stream datum **I[j]**.
3. Write **O[j] = O[j-1] + I[j]**
4. **O[j-1] = O[j]**
5. Go to 1. ; Cycle time is Ci.

As assembler code:

```
BEGIN i
 Out = 0
Loop
 Read I
 Out = Out + I  ;the integration
 Write Out
 Go To Loop
END i
```

Integrating with a calculator: The calculator should have memory. If the calculator has no memory, store to memory would mean write to paper.

1. Set the starting constant in memory.
   (Enter the constant. Store it in memory.)
2. Enter the next number in the Hal stream.
3. Add memory.
4. Store to memory
5. Go to 2.

In a spreadsheet, you will have to set up a column or row to integrate. Suppose the column B is to be integrated. Set up the integrator column in C as:
=C1 + B1 ; replicate that down C. Note that C1 is the integration constant.

As an INode, you must have memory. An INode can count to a number larger than its bit capacity. Like all adders, you simply let it roll. If last O was 200 and I = 150, then new O would be 94 (350 -256).

INodes obey all the rules of calculus without the limitation of requiring a limiting process. kPD = i(kP(D-1)
X = d(i(X)) and N = i(d(N))

Every integrator increases the degree of the incoming Hal stream. The integrator uses the differential of the curve being built as instructions to build the curve.

INode truth tables

I	Out	I	Out
1	1	1	1
1	2	2	3
1	3	3	6

C1 = i(1) ; C1 = 1 2 3 4 5 ...

C2 = i(C1) ; C2 = 1 3 6 10 15 ...
C3 = i(C2) ; C3 = 1 4 10 20 35 ...
...
And so on.

This string of INodes computes every combinatorial sequence. C1 is combinations of N taken 1 at a time. C2 is combinations of N + 2 taken 2 at a time, and so on, to combinations of N + n + k taken k at a time. Note that all n things are produced and we are manipulating k only.

Since an integrator is a counter, INodes can be used whenever you need to time or count some event or condition.

Let s = A z 1 ; s is one if A is zero, else A is zero.

Now timeofs = i(s) ; will count while A is zero and will retain that, since i(0) = x. If A is zero for 5 c times, then timeofs will be 1 2 3 4 5 5 5 5 5 5 5 5 5 ...

This is a cumulative time, since timeofs does not reset. If you need frequency, become an FNode.

Here is the INode code:

```
; BEGIN I Node
 [INIT]
Loop
 [READ I]
;-----------------------------------------------
;
; Begin I function
;
 MOVF        M,W           ; W = M
 ADDWF       I,0           ; W = W + I
 MOVWF       Out           ; Out = W
 MOVWF       M             ; M = W
;
; End I function
;
; Do Output
;
 [WRITE Out]
 GOTO        Loop
;
; end I Node
 END
```

If you need an integration constant, add it externally. For example, i(I) + c = 0 ; is integral with constant.
Feed i(I) into a P node adds another Hal stream and can be any integration constant. Taking the constant out of the node gives you maximum flexibility.

4. An accumulating function - PLUS

Nature -> Sensors -> **Brain** -> Motors -> Nature

PLUS node

You are a node that accumulates. Out = Out + I ; is the action. You are almost an I node.

I	Out	Plus
0	0	0
1	1	1
2	3	3
2	3	5
1	4	6

The difference is you add only if the input is different from the last input.

Here is the PLUS code:

```
; BEGIN PLUS
 [INIT]
Loop
 [READ I]
;--------------------------------------------------
;
; Begin PLUS function
;
 MOVF       I,W          ; W = I
 SUBWF      OldI         ; OldI - W
 BTFSS      STATUS,2     ; I = OldI?
 GOTO       No
 GOTO       Yes
No
 MOVF       M,W          ; W = M
 ADDWF      I,0          ; W = W + I
 MOVWF      M            ; M = W
Yes
 MOVF       M,W          ; W = M
 MOVWF      Out          ; Out = W
 MOVF       I,W          ; W = I
 MOVWF      OldI         ; OldI = W
; End PLUS function
;
; Do Output
;
 [WRITE Out]
 GOTO       Loop
;
; END PLUS
 END
```

4. A decreasing function --- MINUS

Nature -> Sensors -> **Brain** -> Motors -> Nature

MINUS node

You are a node that decreases itself. It is the inverse of the PLUS node. You are almost a D node. You are an un counter.

Out = Out - I ; is the action.

I	Out	Minus
1	-1	0
2	-3	1
2	-3	0
1	-4	-1

Here is the MINUS code:

```
; BEGIN MINUS
 [INIT]
Loop
 [READ I]
;--------------------------------------------------
; BEGIN MINUS function
 MOVF        OldI,W        ; W = OldI
 SUBWF       I,0           ; W = I - W
 BTFSC       STATUS,2      ; W <> 0?
 GOTO        Yes
No                         ; no W is not 0
 MOVF        OldI,W        ; W = OldI
 SUBWF       I,0           ; W = I - W
 MOVWF       M             ; M = W
Yes                        ; yes W is 0
 MOVF        M,W           ; W = M
 MOVWF       Out           ; Out = W
 MOVF        I,W           ; W = I
 MOVWF       OldI          ; OldI = W
;
; END MINUS function
; -------------------------------------------------
[ Write Out ]
; END
```

This is the end of the single input nodes. Now we start with two inputs.

2. S Nodes

We begin the two input nodes. These create Hal Trees. Here is the platform picture:

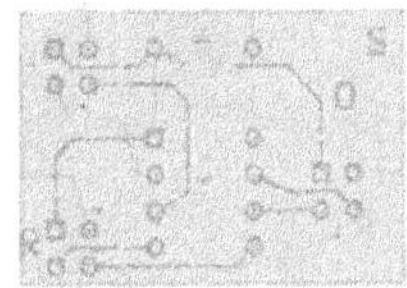

Figure 8 SNodes

Keep this in mind for the code that follows.
All SNodes read L then read R, do a function and write Out. Only the function code is shown for the functions. There is code that is common to all SNodes. The routines are [Init], [Read L and R], and [Write O]. For reference all these are shown here.

```
 [Init]  ;follows
; Setup for 12F629 SNodes
 LIST p=12F629, w=1
; Constants
; Node constants
LC     EQU   05h          ;L control input pin
LD     EQU   04h          ;L data input pin
;
RC     EQU   03h          ;R control input pin
RD     EQU   02h          ;R data input pint
;
OC     EQU   01h          ;O Output control pin
OD     EQU   00h          ;O output data pin
;
; Bank 0 registers
STATUS       EQU   03h
GPIO         EQU   05h    ;I/O port
INTCON       EQU   0Bh
PIR1         EQU   0Ch
TICON        EQU   10h
CMCON        EQU   19h
ADRESH       EQU   1Eh
ADCON        EQU   1Fh
;
; Bank 1 registers
OPTIONR      EQU   81h
TRISIO       EQU   85h
PIE1         EQU   8Ch
PCON         EQU   8Eh
OSCCAL       EQU   90h
WPU          EQU   95h
IOC          EQU   96h
VRCON EQU    99h
EEDATA       EQU   9Ah
EEADR EQU    9Bh
EECON1       EQU   9Ch
EECON2       EQU   9Dh
ADRESL       EQU   9Eh
ANSEL EQU    9Fh
```

```
;
; Variables
L      EQU   20h    ; left input
R      EQU   21h    ; right input
Out    EQU   22h    ; output
D      EQU   23h    ; digit counter
TT     EQU   24h    ; time counter
M      EQU   25h    ; memory
;
 ORG         00h
 BCF         STATUS,5     ;bank0
 CLRF GPIO         ;GPIO = 0
 MOVLW       07h          ; W = 07h
 MOVWF       CMCON ; CMCON = W (comparator off)
 CLRF PIR1         ; PIR1 = 0
 CLRF TICON ; TICON = 0
;
 BSF         STATUS,5     ; STATUS[5] = 1 (bank1)
 CALL 3FFh         ; W = cal (get calibration)
 MOVWF       OSCCAL       ; OSCCAL = W
; do bank1 init
 CLRF OPTIONR      ;option
 CLRF PIE1         ; PIE1 = 0
 CLRF PCON         ; PCON = 0
 CLRF WPU          ; WPU = 0 (Disable weak pull ups)
 CLRF IOC          ; IOC = 0 (disable int on change)
 CLRF VRCON        ; VRCON = 0
; set IO
 MOVLW       3Ch          ; W = 3Ch (5,4,3,2 in 1,0 out)
 MOVWF       TRISIO       ; TRISIO = W
;
 BCF         STATUS,5     ; STATUS[5] = 0 (bank 0)
 CLRF GPIO         ; GPIO = 0
;
Loop      ;Loop label goes here in sequence
 [Read L and R] ;follows When you see Read,
this is the code.
;
```

```
;-------------------------------------------------
ReadL
;Find start
 MOVLW      04h          ; W = 04h *4, 9, 18)
 MOVWF      TT           ; TT = W (bit, half word, whole
word)
CL
 BTFSC      GPIO,LC      ; LC = 0? (look at LC)
 GOTO       ReadL ; [no]
 DECFSZ     TT           ; [yes] TT = TT - 1 is it 0
 GOTO       CL           ; [no]
; found start, read the word.
 CLRF D             ; [yes] D = 0
 CLRF TT            ; TT = 0
 BCF        STATUS,0     ; STATUS[0] = 0
L1
 BTFSC      GPIO,LC      ; LC = 0? )0 bit low?)
 GOTO RDLBit        ; [no], is high
 DECFSZ     TT           ; yes], TT = TT - 1 is it 0?
 GOTO L1            ; [no], not timed out
 GOTO GotL          ; [yes], timed out, give up
; read bit
RDLBit
 BTFSS      GPIO,LD      ; LD = 1? (test bit)
 GOTO       ZeroL ; [no]
 BSF  L,7           ; [yes] L[7] = 1 (is one, move it to
L)
 GOTO       ComL         ;
ZeroL
 BCF  L,7           ; L[7] = 0 (move bit to L)
 NOP                     ; W = W
ComL
 INCF       D            ; D = D + 1 (next bit)
 BTFSC      D,3          ; d[3] = 0? (bits done?)
 GOTO       GotL         ; [no]
 BCF        STATUS,0     ; [yes] STATUS[0] = 0
 RRF  L,1           ; L[j] = L[j+1]
 GOTO       L1           ; Do until bits are done
GotL
```

```
;-------------------------------------------------
ReadR
;Find start
 MOVLW      04h          ; W = 04h (4, 9, 18)
 MOVWF      TT           ; TT = W (bit, halfword, whole
word)
CR
 BTFSC      GPIO,RC      ; RC = 0? (look at RC)
 GOTO       ReadR        ; [no]
 DECFSZ     TT           ; [yes] TT = TT - 1 is it 0?
 GOTO       CR           ; [no] (5*TT)
; found start, read the word.
 CLRF D            ; [yes] D = 0
 CLRF TT           ; TT = 0
 BCF        STATUS,0     ; STATUS[0] = 0
R1
 BTFSC      GPIO,RC      ; is RC = 0? (0 bit low?)
 GOTO RDRBit       ; [no] go read
 DECFSZ     TT           ; [yes] TT = TT - 1 is it 0?
 GOTO R1           ; [no]
 GOTO GotR         ; [yes] timed out
; read bit
RDRBit
 BTFSS      GPIO,RD      ; RD = 1? test bit
 GOTO       ZeroR        ; [no] is zero
 BSF  R,7          ; [yes] R[7] = 1 ( move it to R)
 GOTO       ComR         ;
ZeroR
 BCF  R,7          ; R[7] = 0 (move bit to R)
 NOP               ; W = W
; bit read.
ComR
 INCF       D            ; D = D + 1
 BTFSC      D,3          ; D[3] = 0? (bits done?)
 GOTO       GotR         ; [no]
 BCF        STATUS,0     ; [yes] STATUS[0] = 0
 RRF  R,1          ; R[j] = R[j+1]
 GOTO       R1           ; Do until bits are done
GotR
```

```
;----------------------------------------
; the SNode function goes here.
; ----------------------------------------
; [Write Out] follows:
;
 MOVLW      014h        ; W = 14h (make start time)
 MOVWF      TT          ; TT = W
DTime
 NOP                    ; W = W
 NOP                    ; W = W
 DECFSZ     TT          ; TT = TT - 1, is it 0?
 GOTO DTime       ; [no]
 CLRF       D           ; [yes] D = 0
WriteO
 BCF  GPIO,OC     ; OC = 0 (set control off)
 BCF  GPIO,OD     ; OD = 0 (and data)
; write bit
 BTFSS      Out,0       ; Out[0] = 1? (test bit of Out)
 GOTO       ZeroO       ; [no]
 BSF  GPIO,OD     ; [yes] OD = 1 (send one)
 GOTO       ComO        ;
ZeroO
 BCF  GPIO,OD     ; OD = 0 (send zero)
 NOP                    ; W = W
; bit written
ComO
 BSF  GPIO,OC     ; OC = 1 (set control on)
 NOP                    ; W = W
 NOP                    ; W = W
 BCF  STATUS,0    ; STATUS[0] = 0
 RRF  Out,1       ; Out[j] = Out[j+1]
 INCF       D           ; D = D + 1
 BTFSS      D,3         ; D[3] = 1? (test count)
 GOTO       WriteO      ;  [no] or continue if count
done
 BCF  GPIO,OC     ; [yes] OC = 0 (set control off)
 BCF  GPIO,OD     ; OD = 0 (set data off between words)
 GOTO       Loop
;end node
 END
```

Conventional or stream Algebra nodes

3. Adding Hal Streams --- P node

Nature -> Sensors -> **Brain** -> Motors -> Nature

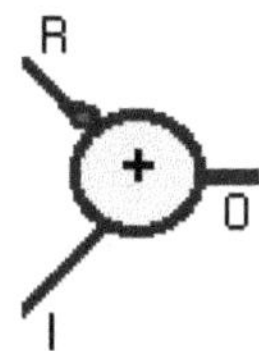

PNode

Out = L + R

You are a P node. **Out = L + R.** You do the + operation and the = operation. You have two motors and a sensor. You have two synapses and an axon.

Inside the P node, you have two numeric displays, one labeled **L** and the other labeled **R**. **L** and **R** come from sensors, real or virtual. To you, L and R are motors that read Hal-Streams. You, the P node, cannot know whether the HalStreams originate from sensors or other nodes. Your job is to mash two HalStreams together and produce the Hal stream Out. The operation of a P node is:

Out = L + R ;Out[Future] = I[Present] + R[Present]

1. Observe the **L[Present]** Hal stream datum.
2. Add the **R[Present]** Hal stream datum.
3. Write **Out[Future] = L[Present] + R[Present]**.
1. Go to 1. Cycle time is Cp.

As assembler code:

```
BEGIN P
Loop
 Read L
 Read R
 Out = L + R
 Write Out
 Go To Loop
END P
```

In a spreadsheet you can add any cell to any other cell.
= A2 + G3

PNode truth tables

L	R	O
-1	-1	-2
-1	0	-1
-1	1	0
0	-1	-1
0	0	0
0	1	1
1	-1	0
1	0	1
1	1	2

L	R	O
0	0	0
0	1	1
0	2	2
1	0	1
1	1	2
1	2	3
2	0	2
2	1	3
2	2	4

A P node, as with every two input HalNode, is two virtual motors, from reading two HalStreams, and a virtual sensor from writing a HalStream. Here, in the brain, all HalStreams can be assumed abstract and dimensionless. It should be noted that L and R are instructions from nature, which includes the rest of the brain.

As a P node, you can compute a number larger than our bit capacity. If that happens then you simply let the wheel roll and the datum on the O Hal stream will be O - b. Example:
L = 200 and R = 150. Then O = 94. (350 - 256)

Combine a P node with an NNode and you can make a C node.

Here is the P node function code:

```
; program for P nodes
; INTRC osc: I/O
; All pins except power and ground are I/O. GP3 input
only
; Out = L + R
; Begin P node
 [Init]
Loop
 [Read L and R]
;--------------------------------------------------
;
; Begin PNode function
;
 MOVF       R,W          ; W = R
 ADDWF      L,0          ; W = W + L
 MOVWF      Out          ; Out = W
;
; End PNode function
;




; Do Output
;----------------------------------------
 [Write Out]
; Cycle data
 GOTO        Loop    ;
; End PNode
```

END

3. Comparing HalStreams – C node

Nature -> Sensors -> **Brain** -> Motors -> Nature

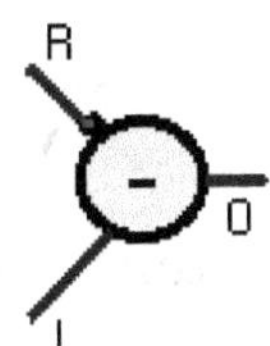

CNode

Out = L - R

You are a C node.

The job of a CNode is to compare two HalStreams. Like the P node, you have two numeric displays that show the HalStreams you are watching. The actions are:

Out = L - R ;Out[Future] = L[Present] - R[Present]

1. Observe the Hal stream datum **L**.
2. Subtract the Hal stream datum **R**.
3. Write the Hal stream datum **Out = L - R**.
4. Go to 1. ; Cycle time is Cc.

As assembler code:

```
CNode
Loop
 Read L
 Read R
 Out = L - R
 Write Out
 Go To Loop
```

In a spreadsheet you can subtract any cell from any other cell.
= G3 - A2

CNode truth tables

L	R	O
0	0	0
0	1	-1
0	2	-2
1	0	1
1	1	0
1	2	-1
2	0	2
2	1	1
2	2	0

L	R	O
-1	-1	0
-1	0	-1
-1	1	-2
0	-1	1
0	0	0
0	1	-1
1	-1	2
1	0	1
1	1	0

C node gets the same result whether it is fed an integer or an offset binary pattern. So it converts everything into an integer.

As in all two input nodes, a C node is two virtual motors and a virtual sensor or two virtual synapses and a virtual axon.

All the theorems of Boolean algebra can be extended to work on HalStreams without restriction. (HalStreams replace bits and arithmetic replaces logic. Unfortunately most switching algebra is to compensate for bit limitations, so very little applies to HalStreams. However work has not even started on ruining Hal algebra.)

Subtraction, like differentiation can change Hal stream types. Subtraction, in a Hal stream is spatial differentiation. This gives us another view of differentiation. We are accustomed to differentiation in time. In space, differentiation covers length. The first derivative looks at one spot, the second looks at two spots and the nth looks at n spots. When CNodes make HalTrees, each column of the tree is the differential of the column before it, since time is along the columns.

There is no exact mechanical analogy for any C node. Mechanics requires units. You can make mechanical torque differentials or force differentials and so on, but there are no abstract mechanisms that can combine into HalTrees.

To see how a C node works, automate a number wheel. Fix it so you can put in a number, and the wheel will rotate to match the number. Create two sensors, one to read the number on the wheel (W), the other to read the number you put in (K).

Make a motor to run the clicker on the wheel (Click). The equation is: Click = K - W

Suppose W is sitting on 5 and you put in 9. Click starts at 4 and starts clicking. You need 4 clicks to get from 5 to 9. But a CNode is more subtle than that.

The first click is from 5 to 6. Now Click is at 3. New instructions have been supplied. That is the effect of continuous action.

Click	K	W	Action
4	9	5	One click
3	9	6	One click
2	9	7	One click
1	9	8	One click
0	9	9	Done

The C node, when in a feedback situation will always count down like this. It will ignore ambient changes in inputs and its last instruction to a motor is always 1 and then 0 to stop.

Here is the C Node code:

```
; program for C nodes
; INTRC osc: I/O
; All pins except power and ground are I/O. GP3 in
; put only
; Out = L - R
; Begin C node
 [Init]
Loop
 [Read L and R]
;---------------------------------------------
;
```

```
; Begin CNode function
;
 MOVF       R,W          ; W = R
 SUBWF      L,0          ; W = L - W
 MOVWF      Out          ; Out = W
;
; End CNode function
;
;------------------------------------------
;
 [Write O]
;
 GOTO Loop   ;
;
; end C Node
 END
```

3. Choosing the Largest Hal stream -- O Node

Nature -> Sensors -> **Brain** -> Motors -> Nature

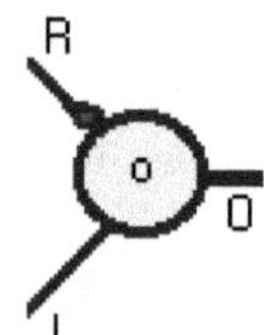

ONode

Out = L o R

You are an ONode. The job of an ONode is to compare two Hal streams and create a new Hal stream with the largest data from either. This is a fuzzy logic OR operation applied to HalStreams instead of sets.

Out = L o R ; Out is equal to L or R

1. Observe the L Hal stream datum
2. Observe the R Hal stream datum
3. Choose the largest
4. Write it to the Out Hal stream
5. Go to 1.

As assembler code:

```
ONode
Loop
 Read L
 Read R
 If L > R then Out = L else Out = R
 Write Out
 Go To Loop
```

In a spreadsheet you can determine the max of any set of cells.
=MAX(A2,C2,G3)
or
=MAX(A2:A42)

ONode truth table b = 3

L	**R**	**Out**
0	0	0
0	1	1
0	2	2
1	0	1
1	1	1
1	2	2
2	0	2
2	1	2
2	2	2

ONodes are a convenience. Sometimes you need to know a value or to lock in a maximum value. If you need to know the single largest of a number of sensors, use a sparse tree of ONodes. A HalTree of ONodes will pick the largest number of any number of inputs, always and continually.

Here is the O Node function code:

```
; program for ONodes
; Out = Max(L,R)
; Begin ONode
 [Init]
Loop
 [Read L and R]
;-----------------------------------------------------
;
; Begin O function MAX(L,R)
;
 MOVF       R,W          ; W = R
 SUBWF      L,0          ; W = L - W
 BTFSS      STATUS,0     ; is W set?
 GOTO        IsR         ; [no] L <= R
 MOVF       L,W          ; [yes] W = L
 GOTO       done         ;
IsR
 MOVF       R,W          ; W = R
done
 MOVWF      Out          ; Out = W
;
; End O function
;
;----------------------------------------
;
 [Write Out]
;
 GOTO       Loop         ;13
;
; end O Node
 END
```

3. Choosing the Smallest Hal stream – A Node

Nature -> Sensors -> **Brain** -> Motors -> Nature

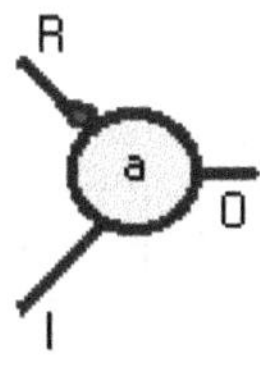

Out = L a R

You are an ANode. The job of an ANode is to compare two Hal streams and create a new Hal stream with the smallest data from either. This is a fuzzy logic AND operation, again using HalStreams instead of sets.

Out = L a R ; Out is equal to L and R

1. Observe the L Hal stream datum
2. Observe the R Hal stream datum
3. Choose the smallest
4. Write it to the Out Hal stream
5. Go to 1.

As assembler code:

```
ANode
Loop
 Read L
 Read R
 If L < R then Out = L else Out = R
 Write Out
 Go To Loop
```

As a spreadsheet function, use the MIN function.

```
=MIN(A2:A43)
```

ANode truth table (b = 3)

L	R	O
0	0	0
0	1	0
0	2	0
1	0	0
1	1	1
1	2	1
2	0	0
2	1	1
2	2	2

Here is the ANode code.

```
; program for A Nodes
; MIN function (L <= R)
; Out = L a R
; O = L a R
; Begin ANode
 [Init]
Loop
 [Read L and R]
;------------------------------------------------------
;
```

```
; Begin A function
;
DoCompare
 MOVF       R,W          ; W = R
 SUBWF      L,0          ; W = L - W
 BTFSC      STATUS,0     ; skip if C clear W neg
 GOTO       IsR
 MOVF       L,W          ; W = L
 GOTO       done         ;
IsR
 MOVF       R,W          ; W = R
done
 MOVWF      Out          ; Out = W
;
; End A function
;
;-----------------------------------------
;
 [Write O]
;
 GOTO       Loop         ;15
;
; end A Node
 END
```

If you need to know the smallest value of a large number of sensors, use a sparse tree of ANodes. It is interesting to note that ANodes will do chemical arithmetic. Given quantities of 2H and O then quantities of water = 2H a O. The quantity of water is measured and limited by the minimum quantities of 2H or O.

3. Multiplying Hal Streams - MPY node

Nature -> Sensors -> **Brain** -> Motors -> Nature

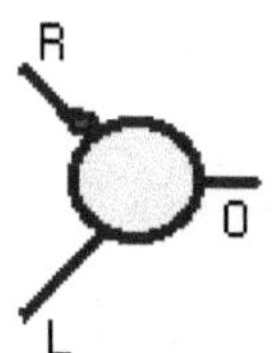

MPY node
Out = L * R

You are a node that multiplies R and L.
Out = L * R ;
MPY is included for completion.

L	R	Out
0	0	0
0	1	0
1	0	0
1	1	1

MPY is the same as AND on binary numbers.

Here is the MPY function code:

```
BEGIN MPY
[ INIT ]
Loop
[ Read L and R ]
; BEGIN MPY function
 MOVF     R,W         ; W = R
 BTFSC    STATUS,2    ;Is R <> 0 ?
 GOTO     Zero        ;no, is zero
 CLRF     Prod        ; Prod = 0
 MOVF     L,W         ; W = L
 BTFSC    STATUS,2    ;is L <> 0 ?
 GOTO     Zero
 MOVF     R,W         ; W = R
 SUBWF    L,W         ; W = L - W
 BTFSS    STATUS,0    ;L < R ?
 GOTO     IsR         ;no, R is bigger
 MOVF     L,W         ;yes, W = L
 GOTO     mpy
IsR
 MOVF     R,W         ; W = R
 MOVWF    temp        ; temp = W
 MOVF     L,W         ; W = L
 MOVWF    R           ; R = W
 MOVF     temp,W      ; W = temp
 MOVWF    L           ; L = W
```

```
mpy
 ADDWF    Prod,1     ; Prod = Prod + W
 DECFSZ   R          ; R = R - 1, is it 0?
 GOTO     mpy        ;no
 MOVF     Prod,W     ;yes, W = Prod
 GOTO     Fini
Zero
 CLRW                ; W = 0
Fini
 MOVWF    Out        ; Out = W
;
; END MPY function
;
 [ Write out ]
GOTO Loop
END MPY
```

3. Dividing Hal Streams ---- DIV node

Nature -> Sensors -> **Brain** -> Motors -> Nature

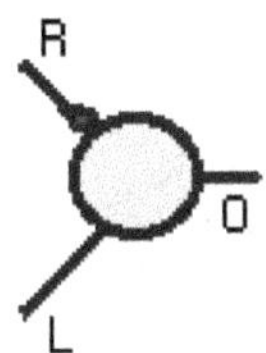

DIV node
Out = L / R

Your are a node that divides L by R

Out = L / R

DIV does an integer divide. It is included for completion of the arithmetic.

L	R	Out
0	0	0
0	1	0
1	0	0
1	1	1

On binary numbers DIV cannot be distinguished from MPY. Note that L/0 = 0 here. (The function would not end if we did not detect divide by 0. The way the code is written, DIV would = 1 but there would never be an output, so you would never see it.)

Here is the DIV function code:

```
BEGIN DIV
[ INIT]
Loop
[ Read L and R }
; BEGIN DIV function
;
 CLRF     Div          ; Div = 0
 MOVF     L,W          ; W = L
 BTFSC    STATUS,2     ;Is L <> 0?
 GOTO     Zero         ; no L = 0
Inc
 INCF     Div          ; yes, L <> 0, Div = Div +
1
DoDiv
 MOVF     R,W          ; W = R
 SUBWF    L,1          ; L = L - W
 BTFSC    STATUS,2     ;result <> 0?
 GOTO     Done         ;
 BTFSC    STATUS,0     ; is 0, is it < 0?
 GOTO     Inc          ; no result > 0, do again
Done
 MOVF     Div,W        ;  yes,  result  <=  0,  W  =
Div
 GOTO     Fini         ; DIV is finished
Zero
 CLRW                  ; W = 0
Fini
 MOVWF    Out          ; Out = W
;
; END DIV function
[ Write Out ]
 GOTO     Loop
END DIV
```

3. A Boolean Logic Hal Node – AND Node

Nature -> Sensors -> **Brain** -> Motors -> Nature

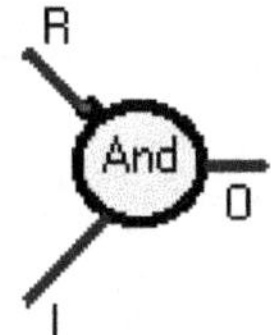

AndNode

Out = L and R

You are a Boolean logic node. You read L and do an and
operation with the mask in R.

Operation
Out = L and R

```
Loop
 Read L
 Read R
 do L and R
 Write Out
 Go to Loop
```

Truth table

L	R	Out
0	0	0
0	1	0
1	0	0
1	1	1

It is convenient to code several things into one number in the detection process. Then use the AndNode to decode.

```
BEGIN AND
[ INIT ]
Loop
 [ Read L and R ]
;-------------------------------------------------------
; BEGIN AND function
;
 MOVF       R,W          ; W = R
 ANDWF      L,0          ; W = L and W
 MOVWF      Out          ; Out = W
;
; END AND function
;----------------------------------------
 [ Write O ]
 GOTO Loop
;
 END AND
```

3, A Boolean Logic Hal Node – OR Node

Nature -> Sensors -> **Brain** -> Motors -> Nature

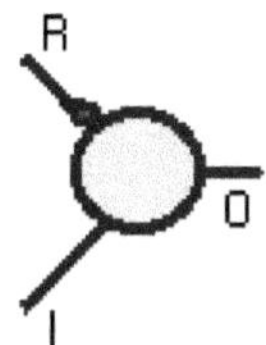

Out = L or R

You are an OR node. When you want to add without carry, use OR instead of Plus.

Operation
Out = L or R

```
Loop
 Read L
 Read R
 do L or R
 Write Out
 Go to Loop
```

Truth table

L	R	Out
0	0	0
0	1	1
1	0	1
1	1	1

Here is the OR function code:

```
BEGIN OR
 [ Init ]
Loop
 [ Read L and R ]
;--------------------------------------------------
;
; BEGIN OR function
;
 MOVF        R,W           ; W = R
 IORWF       L,0           ; W = L OR W
 MOVWF       Out           ; Out = W
;
; END OR function
;-----------------------------------------
 [ Write O ]
 GOTO        Loop
 END OR
```

3. A Boolean Logic Hal Node – NOR

Nature -> Sensors -> **Brain** -> Motors -> Nature

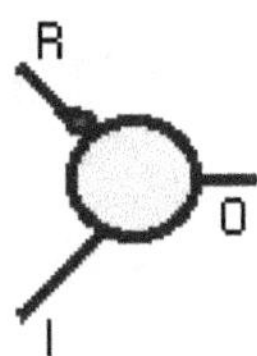

Out = L nor R

You are an NOR node. You are a unique logic function that detects equal and zero. NOR is the complement of OR.

Operation:
Out = L nor R

```
Loop
 Read L
 Read R
 Out = L or R
 Out = complement of Out ;0 -> 1 -> 0
 Write Out
 Go to Loop
```

Truth table

L	R	Out
0	0	1
0	1	0
1	0	0
1	**1**	**0**

; O = L NOR R (bit NOR)

```
BEGIN NOR node (Not OR)
 [Init]
Loop
 [Read L and R]
Loop
;-------------------------------------------------------
; Begin NOR function
;
 MOVF       R,W          ; W = R
 IORWF      L,0          ; W = L OR W
 MOVWF      Out          ; Out = W
 COMF       Out,1        ; Out = Not(Out)
;
; End NOR function
;------------------------------------------
 [Write Out]
 GOTO       Loop
; end NOR
 END
```

3. A Boolean Logic Hal Node – XOR

Nature -> Sensors -> **Brain** -> Motors -> Nature

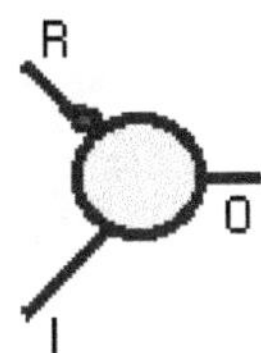

Out = L XOR R

You are an XOR node. You are a unique logic function that detects less than and greater than.

Operation
Out = L xor R

```
Loop
 Read L
 Read R
 Out = L xor R
 Write Out
 Go to Loop
```

Truth table

L	R	Out
0	0	0
0	1	1
1	0	1
1	**1**	**0**

; O = L XOR R (bit NOR)

```
BEGIN XOR node
 [Init]
Loop
```

[Read L and R]

```
Loop
;---------------------------------------
; Begin XOR function
;
 MOVF        R,W          ; W = R
 XORWF       L,0          ; W = L XOR W
 MOVWF       Out          ; Out = W
;
; End XOR function
;---------------------------------------
 [Write Out]
 GOTO        Loop
; end XOR
 END
```

XOR is subtraction without carry.

2. Conditional algebra nodes

3. A Detection HalNode – IS Node

Nature -> Sensors -> **Brain** -> Motors -> Nature

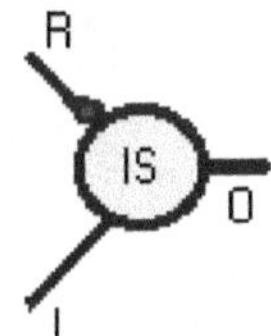

ISNode

Out = L is R

You are an ISNode. You observe the L and R inputs and
if L is equal to R, then make Out = L, else make Out = 0.

Out = L is R ; Out equals L while L equals R, else Out = 0
"is" was chosen as the operator symbol because I do not want two = signs in an equation and it is language equivalent. To say x is y is the same as saying x = y. Of course is means L = R, so we really should say iseq, since we will have isgt and islt for the conditions L > R and L < R respectively.

1. Observe the L Hal stream
2. Compare with the R Hal stream
3. If L = R then make Out = L Else make Out = 0
4. Write Out
5. Go to 1.

As assembler code:

```
BEGIN IS
Loop
 Read L
 Read R
 If L = R then Out = L else Out = 0
 Write Out
 Go To Loop
END IS
```

Spread sheet form

IF(L=R, R, 0) If L is in A2 and R is in B2 then the spreadsheet command is:
=IF(A2=B2,A2,0)

IS Node truth table

L	**R**	**Out**
0	0	0
0	1	0
0	2	0
1	0	0
1	1	1
1	2	0
2	0	0
2	1	0
2	2	2

Here is the IS Node function code.

```
; IS Node
; Out = L is R
;
 [Init]
Loop
 [Read L and R]
;
; Begin IS function
;
 MOVF    R,W      ; W = R
 SUBWF   L,0      ; W = L - W
 BTFSS   3,2      ; if zero, skip
 GOTO    notzero ;
 MOVF    L,W      ; W = L
 GOTO    Fini     ;
notzero
 CLRW             ; W = 0
Fini
 MOVWF   Out      ; Out = W
;
; End IS function
;
 [Write Out]
 GOTO    Loop   ;
; End IS
END
```

A logic HalNode is used for Hal stream logic. They are used when you want an event to occur when some threshold is passed.

Hal algebra is an algebra, so most the rules of algebra can be used.

You should note that the ISNode is a combination CNode and ZNode and should be used when that combination is needed.

3. A Detection HalNode – GT Node

Nature -> Sensors -> **Brain** -> Motors -> Nature

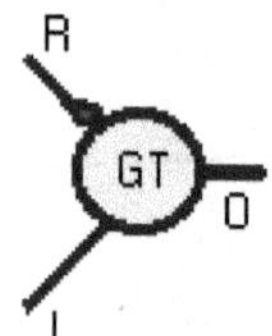

GTNode

Out = L gt R

You are an GT node. You observe the L input and
if L greater than R, then make Out = L-R, else make Out = 0.

Out = L gt R ; Out = L-R if L greater than R, else Out = 0
Out = L > R ; alternate notation

1. Observe the L Hal stream
2. Compare with the R Hal stream
3. If L > R then make Out = L - R Else make Out = 0
4. Write O
5. Go to 1.

As assembler code:

```
BEGIN GT
Loop
 Read L
 Read R
 If L > R then Out = L - R else Out = 0
 Write Out
 Go To Loop
END GT
```

Spread sheet form

IF(L > R, L-R, 0) If L is in A2 and R is in B2 then the spreadsheet command is:

=IF(A2>B2,A2-B2,0)

GTNode truth table

L	**R**	**Out**
0	0	0
0	1	0
0	2	0
1	0	1
1	1	0
1	2	0
2	0	2
2	1	1
2	2	0

```
;GT Node
 [Init]
Loop
 [Read L and R]
;
; Begin GT function
;
 MOVF       R,W           ; W = R
 SUBWF      L,0           ; W = L - W
 MOVWF      DI            ; DI = W
 BTFSS      STATUS,0      ; skip if C set ispos
 GOTO       IsR
IsI                       ; ispos
 MOVF       DI,W          ; W = DI
 GOTO       done
IsR                       ; isneg
 CLRW                     ; W = 0
done
 MOVWF      Out           ; Out = W
;
; End GT function
 [Write Out]
 GOTO Loop
;end
```

3. A Detection HalNode – LT Node

Nature -> Sensors -> **Brain** -> Motors -> Nature

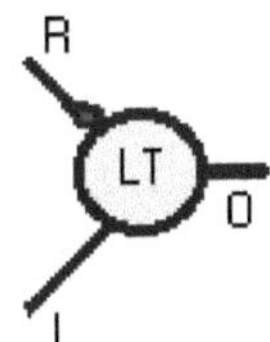

LTNode

Out = L lt R

You are an LT node. You observe the L input and
if L is less than R, then make Out = L-R, else make Out = 0.

Out = L lt R ; Out equals L-R if L less than R, else Out = 0
Out = L < R ; is alternate notation

1. Observe the L Hal stream
2. Compare with the R Hal stream
3. If L < R then make Out = L-R Else make Out = 0
4. Write Out
5. Go to 1.

As assembler code:

```
BEGIN LT
Loop
 Read L
 Read R
 If L < R then Out = L-R else Out = 0
 Write Out
 Go To Loop
END LT
```

Spread sheet form

IF(L < R, L-R, 0) If L is in A2 and R is in B2 then the spreadsheet command is:

```
=IF(A2<B2,A2-B2,0)
```

LTNode truth table

L	R	Out
0	0	0
0	1	0
0	2	0
1	0	0
1	1	0
1	2	1
2	0	0
2	1	0
2	2	0

```
;LT node
; O = L lt R
 [init]
Loop
 [Read L and R]
 ; Begin LT function
;
 MOVF       R,W          ; W = R
 SUBWF      L,0          ; W = L - W
 MOVWF      DI           ; DI = W
 BTFSC      STATUS,0     ; skip if C clear
 GOTO       IsR
IsI                      ; isneg L < R
 MOVF       DI,W         ; W = DI
 GOTO       done
IsR                      ; ispos L > R
 CLRW                    ; W = 0
done
 MOVWF      Out          ; Out = W
;
; End LT function
 [Write Out]
 GOTO Loop
;end Node
 END
```

3. A Detection and memory Hal Node - WEQ

Nature -> Sensors -> **Brain** -> Motors -> Nature

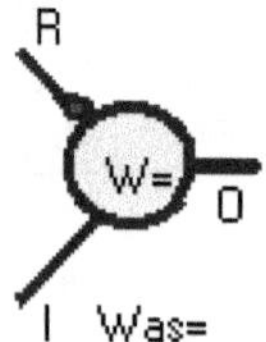

Out = L weq R

You are a WEQ. You observe the L input and
if L was R, then make Out = L and M = L, else make Out = M.

Out = L weq R; Out = L if L was R and M = L, else Out = M

1. Observe the L Hal stream
2. Compare with the R Hal stream
3. If L = R then make M = L and make Out = M
4. Write Out
5. Go to 1.

As assembler code:

```
BEGIN WAS
 M = 0
Loop
 Read L
 Read R
 If L = R then M = L
 Out = M
 Write Out
 Go To Loop
END WAS
```

Spread sheet form
IF(L = R, L, M) If L is in A2 and R is in B2 then the spreadsheet command is:
=IF(A2=B2,A2,A1)

WasEQ truth table

L	R	M	Out
0	0	0	0
0	1	0	0
0	2	0	0
1	0	0	0
1	1	1	1
1	2	1	1
2	0	1	1
2	1	1	1
2	2	1	1

```
;WEQ
; O = L weq R
 [Init]
Loop
 [Read L and R]
;-----------------------------------------------------
; Begin WEQ function
;
 MOVF       R,W          ; W = R
 SUBWF      L,0          ; W = L - W
 BTFSS      STATUS,2     ; is 0?
 GOTO       NoMem        ; [no]
 MOVF L,W           ; [yes], W = L
 MOVWF      M            ; M = W
NoMem
 MOVF M,W           ; W = M
 MOVWF      Out          ; Out = W
;
; End WEQ function
 [Write Out]
 GOTO    Loop   ;
;
 END
; end Node
```

3. A Detection and Memory Hal Node - WGT

Nature -> Sensors -> **Brain** -> Motors -> Nature

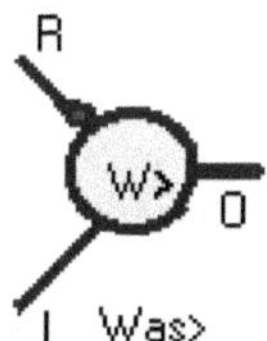

Out = L wgt R

You are a WasGT. You observe the L input and
if L was > R, then make Out = L-R and
M = L-R,
else make Out = M.
Out = L wasgt R ; Out equals L-R if L was > R
and M = L-R and Out = M

1. Observe the L Hal stream
2. Compare with the R Hal stream
3. If L > R then make M = L-R and make Out = M
4. Write Out
5. Go to 1.

As assembler code:

```
BEGIN GT
 M = 0
Loop
 Read L
 Read R
 If L > R then M = L-R
 Out = M
 Write Out
 Go To Loop
END GT
```

Spread sheet form

IF(L > R, L, M) If L is in A2 and R is in B2 then the spreadsheet command is:

=IF(A2>B2,A2-B2,A1)

WasGT truth table

L	R	M	Out
0	0	0	0
0	1	0	0
0	2	0	0
1	0	1	1
1	1	1	1
1	2	1	1
2	0	2	2
2	1	1	1
2	2	1	1

```
;WGT
; Out = L wgt R
 [Init]
Loop
 [Read L and R]
 ;-------------------------------------------
; Begin WGT function
;
 MOVF       R,W         ; W = R
 SUBWF      L,0         ; W = L - W
 MOVWF      DI          ; DI = W
 BTFSS      STATUS,0    ; is > 0?
 GOTO       NoMem       ; [no]
 BTFSC      STATUS,2    ; [yes], is it 0 ?
 GOTO NoMem       ; [yes] it is 0
 MOVF DI,W        ; [no], W = DI
 MOVWF      M           ; M = W
NoMem
 MOVF M,W         ; W = M
 MOVWF      Out         ; Out = W
;
; End WasGT function
;
;-------------------------------------------
 [Write Out]
 GOTO    Loop   ;
;
 END
; end Node
```

3. A Detection and Memory Hal Node - WLT

Nature -> Sensors -> **Brain** -> Motors -> Nature

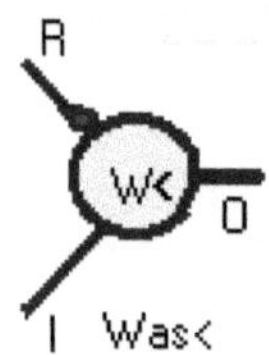

Out = L wlt R

You are a WLT. You observe the L input and
if L was < R, then make Out = L-R and M = L-R, else make Out = M.
Out = L wlt R ; Out equals L-R if L was < R and M = L-R and O = M

1. Observe the L Hal stream
2. Compare with the R Hal stream
3. If L < R then make M = L-R and make Out = M
4. Write Out
5. Go to 1.

As assembler code:

```
BEGIN WLT
 M = 0
Loop
 Read L
 Read R
 If L < R then M = L-R
 Out = M
 Write Out
 Go To Loop
END WLT
```

Spread sheet form
IF(L < R, L, M) If L is in A2 and R is in B2 then the spreadsheet command is:
=IF(A2<B2,A2-B2,A1)

WasLT truth table

L	**R**	**M**	**Out**
0	0	0	0
0	1	-1	-1
0	2	-2	-2
1	0	-2	-2
1	1	-2	-2
1	2	-1	-1
2	0	-1	-1
2	1	-1	-1
2	2	-1	-1

```
; WLT
; Out = L wlt R
 [Init]
Loop
 [Read L and R]
;-----------------------------------
; Begin WLT function
;
 MOVF       R,W          ; W = R
 SUBWF      L,0          ; W = L - W
 MOVWF      DI           ; DI = W
 BTFSC      STATUS,0     ; if <, skip
 GOTO       NoMem        ; [no]
 MOVF       DI,W         ; [yes], W = DI
 MOVWF      M            ; M = W
NoMem
 MOVF       M,W          ; W = M
 MOVWF      Out          ; Out = W
;
; End WLT function
 [ Write Out ]
 GOTO    Loop   ;
;
 END
```

2. Conditional Switching algebra nodes

3. A Conditional Switch Hal Node – L Node

Nature -> Sensors -> **Brain** -> Motors -> Nature

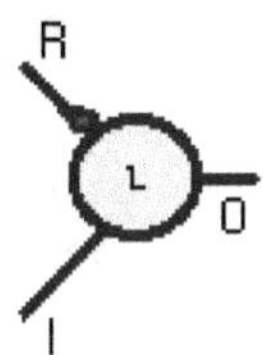

LNode

Out = L l R

You are a L Node. Your job is to watch your L input and divert R into Out while it is less than zero.
Keep Out = 0 otherwise.

Out = L l R ; is the infix notation.

```
Start:
     Out = 0   ; Default status
     While L < 0 Out = R
     Go to Start
```

Assembler code is more like:

```
BEGIN L
Loop
 Read L
 Read R
 If L < 0 then Out = R else Out = 0
 Write Out
 Go To Loop
END L
```

Spread sheet form

IF(L<0, R, 0) Let L be in A2 and R be in B2. Then the spreadsheet command is:

```
=IF(A2<0,B2,0)
```

LNode truth table

Out = L l R

L	R	Out
-1	-1	-1
-1	0	0
-1	1	1
0	-1	0
0	0	0
0	1	0
1	-1	0
1	0	0
1	1	0

Note that R is unspecified. R can be anything from, a constant representing a code, to a complex Hal stream.

LNodes do not make combinatorial trees. An LNode is applied when a CNode is used as an object detector. Here a negative is the signal of detection. The LNode converts the signal of detection into a code of action. The first LNode says, "Here is the property of an object," if an object is detected, and says, "There is no object," otherwise.

All these nodes, Z, G and L are conditional switches, switching data on condition.

```
;-----------------------------------------------
;
; Begin L function
;
 BTFSS   L,7       ; is L < 0?
 Goto    notMinus  ; [no]
 MOVF    R,W       ; [yes], W = R
 GOTO    POUT      ;
notMinus
 CLRW              ; W = 0
POUT
 MOVWF   Out       ; Out = W
;
; End L function
;---------------------------------------
 [ Write Out ]
 GOTO    Loop   ;
;
; end Node
 END
```

3. A Conditional Switch Hal Node – G Node

Nature -> Sensors -> **Brain** -> Motors -> Nature

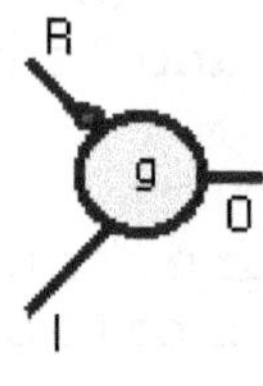

GNode

Out = L g R

You are a GNode. Your job is to watch your L input and divert R into Out while it is Greater than zero.
Keep Out = 0 otherwise.
You are arithmetic logic, not Boolean logic.

Out = L g R ; is the infix notation.

```
Start:
     Out = 0    ; Default status
     While L > 0 Out = R
     Go to Start
```

Assembler code is more like:

```
GNode
Loop
 Read L
 Read R
 If L > 0 then Out = R else Out = 0
 Write Out
 Go To Loop
```

Spread sheet form

IF(L>0, R, 0) Let L be in A2 and R be in B2. Then the spreadsheet command is:
=IF(A2>0,B2,0)

GNode truth table

Out = L g R

L	R	Out
-1	-1	0
-1	0	0
-1	1	0
0	-1	0
0	0	0
END		
0	1	0
1	-1	-1
1	0	0
1	1	1

Note that R is unspecified. R can be anything from, a constant representing a code, to a complex Hal stream.

G Nodes do not make combinatorial trees. A G Node is applied when a CNode is used as an object detector. Here a positive is the signal of detection. The GNode converts the signal of detection into a code of action. The first GNode says, "Here is the property of an object," if an object is detected, and says, "There is no object," otherwise.

```
GNode
 Init
Loop
 Read L
 Read R
;-----------------------------------------------------
;
; Begin G function
;
 MOVF       L,W          ; W = L
 BTFSC      STATUS,2     ; is L <> 0?
 GOTO       notPlus      ;[yes] L is 0
 BTFSC      L,7          ;[no], is L > 0?
 Goto       notPlus      ;[no]
 MOVF       R,W          ;[yes], W = R
 GOTO       POUT         ;
notPlus
 CLRW                    ; W = 0
POUT
 MOVWF   Out             ; Out = W
;
; End GNode function
;----------------------------------------
 [ Write Out ]
 GOTO    Loop   ;
;
; end Node
 END
```

3. A Conditional Switch Hal Node – Z Node

Nature -> Sensors -> **Brain** -> Motors -> Nature

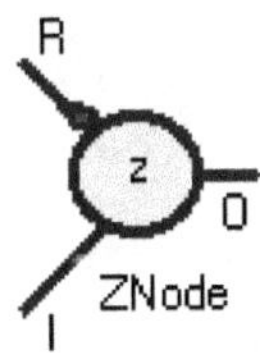

Out = L z R

You are a z Node. Your job is to watch your L input and divert R into Out while it is equal to zero.
Keep Out = 0 otherwise.

Out = L z R ; is the infix notation.

```
Start:
     Out = 0   ; Default status
     While L = 0 Out = R
     Go to Start
```

Assembler code is more like:

```
BEGIN Z
Loop
 Read L
 Read R
 If L = 0 then Out = R else Out = 0
 Write Out
 Go To Loop
END Z
```

Spread sheet form

IF(L=0, R, 0) Let L be in A2 and R be in B2. Then the spreadsheet command is:
=IF(A2=0,B2,0)

Z Node truth table

Out = L z R

L	R	Out
-1	-1	0
-1	0	0
-1	1	0
0	-1	-1
0	0	0
0	1	1
1	-1	0
1	0	0
1	1	0

Note that R is unspecified. R can be anything from, a constant representing a code, to a complex Hal stream.

Z Nodes do not make combinatorial trees. A Z Node is applied when a CNode is used as an object detector. Here a zero is the signal of detection. The Z Node converts the signal of detection into a code of action. The first Z Node says, "Here is the property of an object," if an object is detected, and says, "There is no object," otherwise.

All these nodes, Z, G and L are conditional switches, switching data on condition.

```
;-----------------------------------------------
;
; Begin Z function
;
 BTFSS   STATUS,2 ; is L = 0?
 Goto    notZero ; [no]
 MOVF    R,W      ; [yes], W = R
 GOTO    POUT     ;
notZero
 CLRW             ; W = 0
POUT
 MOVWF   Out      ; Out = W
;
; End Z function
;-----------------------------------------
 [ Write Out ]
 GOTO    Loop   ;
;
; end Node
 END
```

3. A Conditional Switch Hal Node – DL Node

Nature -> Sensors -> **Brain** -> Motors -> Nature

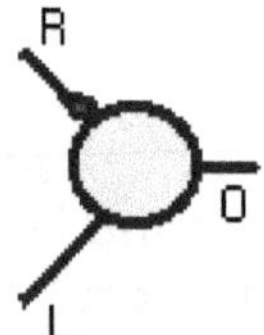

DL Node

Out = L dl R

You are a DL Node. Your job is to watch your L input and divert R into Out while d(L) is less than zero.
Keep Out = 0 otherwise.
You are arithmetic logic, not Boolean logic.

Out = L dl R ; is the infix notation.

```
Start:
     Read L
     Read R
     If d(L) < 0 Then Out = R else Out = 0
     Go to Start
```

Assembler code is more like:

```
DL Node
 OldL = 0
Loop
 Read L
 Read R
 DI = L - OldL
 If DI < 0 then Out = R else Out = 0
 Write Out
 OldL = L
 Go To Loop
```

DL Node truth table

Out = L dl R

L	**R**	**DL**	**Out**
-1	1	0	0
-1	1	0	0
-1	1	0	0
0	1	1	0
0	1	-1	1

```
 BEGIN DL Node
 [ Init ]
 OldL = 0
Loop
 [ Read L ]
 [ Read R ]
;-------------------------------------------------------
;
; Begin dl function
;
 MOVF        L,W           ; W = L
 SUBWF       OldL,0        ; W = W - OldL
 BTFSC       STATUS,2      ; is W <> 0?
 GOTO notPlus     ;[yes] W is 0
 BTFSC       L,7           ;[no], is L > 0?
 Goto        notPlus       ;[no]
 MOVF        R,W           ;[yes], W = R
 GOTO        POUT          ;
notPlus
 CLRW                      ; W = 0
POUT
 MOVWF    Out              ; Out = W
;
; End GNode function
;-------------------------------------------
 [ Write Out ]
 GOTO     Loop    ;
;
; end Node
 END
```

3. A Conditional Switch Hal Node – DG Node

Nature -> Sensors -> **Brain** -> Motors -> Nature

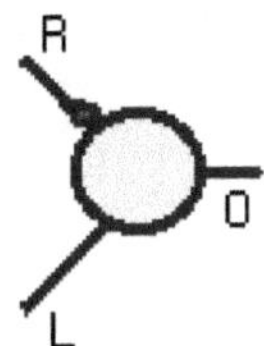

DG Node

Out = L dg R

You are a DG Node. Your job is to watch your L input and divert R into Out while d(L) is Greater than zero.
Keep Out = 0 otherwise.
You are arithmetic logic, not Boolean logic.

Out = L dg R ; is the infix notation.

```
Start:
     Read L
     Read R
     If d(L) > 0 Then Out = R Else Out = 0
     Go to Start
```

Assembler code is more like:

```
GNode
OldL = 0
Loop
 Read L
 Read R
 DL = L - OldL
 If DL > 0 then Out = R else Out = 0
 Write Out
 Go To Loop
```

DG Node truth table

Out = L dg R

L	R	DL	Out
-1	1	0	0
-1	1	0	0
-1	1	0	0
0	1	1	1
0	1	0	0

Note that R is unspecified. R can be anything from, a constant representing a code, to a complex Hal stream.

```
BEGIN DG Node
[ Init ]
 Di = 0
 [ Read I ]
 [ Read R ]
;-----------------------------------------------
;
; Begin DGNode function
;
 MOVF       Dm,W          ; W = Dm
 SUBWF      I,0           ; W = I - W
 MOVWF      Di            ; Di = W
 MOVF       Di,W          ; W = Di
 BTFSS      STATUS,0      ; is Di > 0?
 GOTO       NotZero       ; [no] make O = 0
 MOVF       R,W           ; [yes] W = R
 BTFSS      STATUS,2      ; is R = 0?
 GOTO       Comm          ; [no]
 MOVLW      1h            ; [yes] W = 1
 GOTO       Comm
NotZero
 CLRW                     ; W = 0
Comm
 MOVWF      Out           ; Out = W
 MOVF       I,W           ; W = I
 MOVWF      Dm            ; Dm = W
;
; End DG Node function
;
; Do Output
 [ Write Out ]
 GOTO    Loop
;
; end DG Node
 END
```

3. A Conditional Switch Hal Node – DZ Node

Nature -> Sensors -> **Brain** -> Motors -> Nature

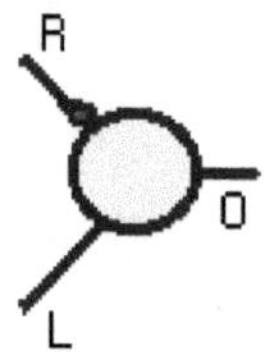

Out = L dz R

You are a DZ Node. Your job is to watch your L input and divert R into Out while d(L) is equal to zero.
Keep Out = 0 otherwise.
You are arithmetic logic, not Boolean logic.

Out = L dz R ; is the infix notation.

```
Start:
     Read L
     Read R
     If d(L) = 0 Then Out = R Else Out = 0
     Go to Start
```

Assembler code is more like:

```
DZ Node
 M = 0
Loop
 Read L
 Read R
 If L - M = 0 then Out = R else Out = 0
 Write Out
 M = L
 Go To Loop
```

DZ Node truth table

Out = L dz R

L	**R**	**d(L)**	**Out**
-1	1	0	0
-1	1	0	1
-1	1	0	1
0	1	1	0
0	1	0	1

Note that R is unspecified. R can be anything from, a constant representing a code, to a complex Hal stream.

```
BEGIN DZ Node
 Init
 OldL = 0
Loop
 Read L
 Read R
;---------------------------------------------------
; Begin DZ Node function
;
 MOVF         Dm,W          ; W = Dm
 SUBWF        L,0           ; W = L - W
 MOVWF        Di            ; Di = W
 MOVF         Di,W          ; W = Di
 BTFSS        STATUS,2      ; is Di = 0?
 GOTO         NotZero       ; [no] make O = 0
 MOVF         R,W           ; [yes] W = R
 BTFSS        STATUS,2      ; is R = 0?
 GOTO         Comm          ; [no]
 MOVLW        1h            ; [yes] W = 1
 GOTO         Comm
NotZero
 CLRW                       ; W = 0
Comm
 MOVWF        Out           ; Out = W
 MOVF         L,W           ; W = L
 MOVWF        Dm            ; Dm = W
; End DZ Node function
;-------------------------------------------
 [ Write Out ]
 GOTO     Loop    ;
;
; end Node
 END
```

2. Motors

3. Reading a Hal stream - Motors

Nature -> Sensors -> Brain -> **Motors** -> Nature

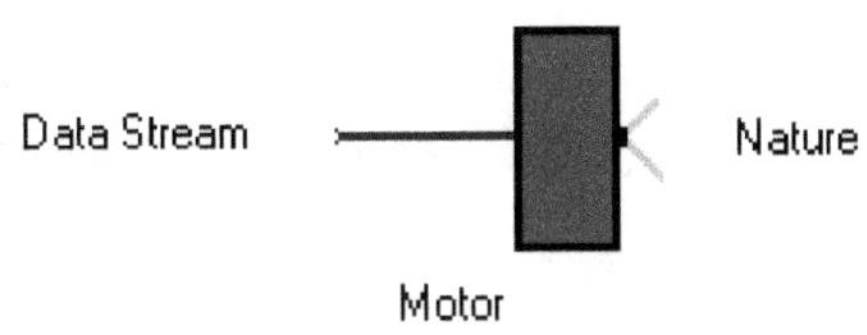

Motor = I

You are a real motor controller. You watch the I input and do what it says. You read the data. You put units and meaning to the Hal stream. You are the decoder of this Hal stream. I is a synapse on a muscle, coming from some HalTree of some axon.

The job of a motor is to convert a Hal stream into an action. You are the final reader of a Hal stream although you do not consume it. It can continue beyond you. But if a Hal stream ends, it ends with a motor. A HalTree ending in a motor is called a command tree. The size of the HalTree determines the possible actions of the motor. All that is connected to the motor is a function.

M = I[Present]

The operation of the motor is:

1. Observe the Hal stream.
2. Use the quantity to run an action in the direction and amount indicated by the number in the Hal stream.
3. Go to 1. ; Cycle time is Cm.

Assembler code is like:

```
Loop
 Read I
 DO I         ;with 8 bits you have 256 possi-
ble actions.
 Go To Loop
```

Operation 2, or DO I, can be simple or complex and can only be specified when the design process is complete. Operation 2 must be specified. In the virtual motors of the other nodes, operation 2 is to simply put the input into a memory. In a CNode, for example, the R input motor makes a twos complement number of the number coming in on the cable. The I input simply puts the input number into a register.

Motors require time to cycle. The speed of the action that is produced is usually slower than the cycle time of the Hal stream. Fortunately, nature has cycles of every scale and most actions of animals and Robots are very slow.

The task of every motor is to decide what to do with the input integer. We can make conventions here by always making minus numbers go left or counter clockwise or backward and so on. It is no big deal. You can always add an inverter to fix this.

It is in the motor that meaning is given to Hal stream variables. The purpose of the motor is to give expression to the semantic of the Hal stream variable. The construction of a motor that is a body part is still an art and requires all the technology available to the engineer. In time, you will be able to classify motors as to function so you can buy them off the shelf.

A real motor sits half in the brain and half in the world. A motor decodes and makes concrete the actions of the brain. Here you add units, dimensions and goals to the abstract Hal stream from the brain.

There are intermediate nodes between nodes and motors. In the computer analogy, these are drivers. The first is MoNode which converts number into pulsed voltage via an H-bridge. I -> velocity. Here is the code for MoNode:

```
; program for MoNodes
; Integer -> pulse width for motors.
; Out = pulse and direction
; M1 = Not(Run) = Not(OD)
; M2 = Not(Dir) = Not(OC)
; M1 = 1, M2 = 0 current direction is plus
; M2 = 1, M1 = 0 current direction is minus
;
; Begin MoNode
; Setup for 12F629 MoNodes
;
 LIST p=12F629, w=1
; Constants
MX     EQU   07Fh
; Node constants
IC     EQU   05h    ;I control input pin
ID     EQU   04h    ;I data input pin
;
RC     EQU   03h    ;R control input pin
RD     EQU   02h    ;R data input pint
;
OC     EQU   01h    ;O Output control pin
OD     EQU   00h    ;O output data pin
;
; Bank 0 registers
TMR0         EQU   02h
STATUS       EQU   03h
GPIO         EQU   05h    ;I/O port
INTCON       EQU   0Bh
PIR1         EQU   0Ch
TICON        EQU   10h
CMCON        EQU   19h
ADRESH       EQU   1Eh
ADCON        EQU   1Fh
;
```

```
; Bank 1 registers
OPTIONR      EQU   81h
TRISIO       EQU   85h
PIE1         EQU   8Ch
PCON         EQU   8Eh
OSCCAL       EQU   90h
WPU          EQU   95h
IOC          EQU   96h
VRCON        EQU   99h
EEDATA       EQU   9Ah
EEADR        EQU   9Bh
EECON1       EQU   9Ch
EECON2       EQU   9Dh
ADRESL       EQU   9Eh
ANSEL        EQU   9Fh
;
; Variables
I            EQU   20h    ;var starts
Out          EQU   21h
D            EQU   22h
TT           EQU   23h
P            EQU   24h
RT           EQU   25h
OT           EQU   26h
Ton          EQU   27h
ISign        EQU   28h
temp         EQU   29h
;
 ORG         00h
 BCF         STATUS,5     ;bank0
 CLRF GPIO
 MOVLW       07h
 MOVWF       CMCON        ;comparator off
 CLRF PIR1
 CLRF TICON
;
 BSF         STATUS,5     ;bank1
 CALL 3FFh         ;get calibration
 MOVWF       OSCCAL       ;set it
```

```
; do bank1 init
 CLRF OPTIONR       ;option
 CLRF PIE1
 CLRF PCON
 CLRF WPU           ;Disable weak pull ups
 CLRF IOC           ;disable interrupt on change
 CLRF VRCON
; set IO
 MOVLW      3Ch           ;5,4,3,2 in 1,0 out
 MOVWF      TRISIO
;
 BCF        STATUS,5      ;bank 0
 CLRF GPIO
;
Loop
;
```

```
;----------------------------------------
; I input for TNodes, MoNodes
ReadI
;Find start
 MOVLW      04h           ;4, 9, 18
 MOVWF      TT            ;bit, halfword, whole word
CI
 BTFSC      GPIO,IC       ;1 look at IC
 GOTO ReadI               ;2 is on
 DECFSZ     TT            ;3
 GOTO CI                  ;4 5*TT
; found start, read the word.
 CLRF D             ;start with bit 0
 CLRF TT            ;
 BCF        STATUS,0      ;
I1
 BTFSC      GPIO,IC       ;0 bit Low?
 GOTO RDIBit        ;1 no, is high, go read
 DECFSZ     TT            ;2 yes, time it
 GOTO I1            ;3 try again
 GOTO GotI          ; give up
; read bit
RDIBit
 BTFSS      GPIO,ID       ;2 yes, test bit
 GOTO ZeroI         ;3 is zero
 BSF        I,7           ;4 is one, move it to I
 GOTO ComI          ;5
ZeroI
 BCF        I,7           ;4 move bit to I
 NOP                      ;5
; bit read.
ComI
 INCF D             ;7 next bit
 BTFSC      D,3           ;8 bits done?
 GOTO GotI          ;9
 BCF        STATUS,0      ;10
 RRF        I,1           ;11
 GOTO I1            ;11 Do until bits are done
GotI
;--------------------------------------------------------
;
```

```
; Begin MoNode function
;
 MOVF I,W            ; W = I
 BTFSC      STATUS,2      ;Zero?
 GOTO CZ             ;yes, skip all
 BTFSS      I,7           ;no, If input is plus
 GOTO       IsPlus        ;0 is plus
; do minus
 COMF I,1            ; I = Not(I)
 INCF I              ; I = I + 1, making twos complement
 BSF        ISign,7       ; ISign,7 = 1, set sign -
 GOTO ComO           ; yes, go to time test
;
IsPlus
 BCF        ISign,7       ; ISign,7 = 0, set sign +
ComO
; Ton = RT - (MX-I)
 MOVF TMR0,W         ; W = TMRO
 MOVWF      RT            ; RT = W , readI cycle time
 CLRF TMR0           ; TMR0 = 0
 MOVF RT,W           ; W = RT
 MOVWF      Ton           ; Ton = W, start Ton at RT
 MOVLW      MX            ; W = MX
 MOVWF      temp          ; temp = W
 MOVF I,W            ; W = I
 SUBWF      temp          ; W = temp - W
 MOVF temp,W         ; W = temp
 SUBWF      Ton           ; Ton = RT -(MX-I)
 MOVF TMR0,W         ; W = TMR0
 ADDWF      Ton           ; Ton = Ton + W
 ADDWF      RT            ; RT = RT + W
 CLRF TMR0           ; TMR0 = 0, Time is now in OT
;
 BTFSS      ISign,7       ; is I minus
 GOTO PP             ; no,
;
 BCF        GPIO,OD       ;yes
 BSF        GPIO,OC       ;set minus pulse on 1 0 OC ----
---
 GOTO CP             ;
```

```
PP
 BCF        GPIO,OC     ;
 BSF        GPIO,OD     ;set plus pulse on  0 1 OD ----
-
CP
 MOVF TMR0,W       ; W = TMR0
 MOVWF      temp        ; temp = W
 MOVF Ton,W ; W = Ton
 SUBWF      temp        ; TMR0 - Ton
 BTFSS      STATUS,0    ; equal or >?
 GOTO CP           ; no, OT < Ton
;
CZ
 BCF        GPIO,OC     ; yes, Pulse off ----------
 BCF        GPIO,OD
 MOVF TMR0,W       ; W = TMR0
 MOVWF      OT          ; OT = W compute OT for info
and test
 CLRF TMR0         ; TMR0 = 0
;
; End MoNode function
;
 GOTO       Loop
 END
; end MoNode
```

There is also an SMNode that converts number into a servo timed pulse. I -> position. Here is the code.

```
; program for SMNodes Version
; Use TNode board
; Integer -> Timed pulse for servo
; Out = pulse cycle
; Node is:
; 4 Mhz is Megacycles/sec 4000000
; 4 clock cycles per pic code line.
; 1 Microsecond/cycle .0000001 sec/cycle
; 1 millisecond = .001 sec = 1000 cycles
; Vcount for variable time
; Servo is:                        In   comp
; 1 millisecond puts servo full CCW input = -128 0
; 1.5 millisecond puts servo at center input = 0 128
; 2 milliseconds puts servo full CW  input = 127 255
; Wait 20 milliseconds for next cycle.
; Rule is:
;loop
; turn on pulse
; By default produce 1.0 ms
; I produces up to 1.0 ms     5 cc = 1 int = .005 ms
; turn off pulse        1000 cc = 200 int = 1.00 ms
; wait 20 ms                  cc = int*5 = ms*0.001
; goto loop
; I    pulse      hex
; -100 1 ms 9C
; -99  1.005 ms   9D
; 0    1.5 ms     0
; 1    1.505 ms   1
; 100  2 ms 64
; Begin SMNode
```

```
;       Constants
Ctime EQU   D'32'          ;feeds CCount makes 100
Dtime EQU   D'10'          ;10 Decade
DVTime       EQU   D'5'          ;5 VCount = 5*In
BigTime      EQU   D'19' ;19 was 20, now incl inp
moff         EQU   80h           ;-128
;
IC           EQU   05h   ;input port pins
ID           EQU   04h
;
OD           EQU   00h   ;pulse pin
; registers
; Bank 0
STATUS       EQU   03h
GPIO         EQU   05h
INTCON       EQU   0Bh
PIR1         EQU   0Ch
TICON EQU   10h
CMCON EQU   19h
ADRESH       EQU   1Eh
ADCON EQU   1Fh
;
; Bank 1
OPTIONR      EQU   81h
TRISIO       EQU   85h
PIE1         EQU   8Ch
PCON         EQU   8Eh
OSCCAL       EQU   90h
WPU          EQU   95h
IOC          EQU   96h
VRCON EQU   99h
EEDATA       EQU   9Ah
EEADR EQU   9Bh
EECON1       EQU   9Ch
EECON2       EQU   9Dh
ADRESL       EQU   9Eh
ANSEL EQU   9Fh
```

```
;     Variables
I            EQU   020h          ;Raw input variable
Tcount       EQU   021h          ;20 ms counter
BigCount     EQU   022h          ;20 ms inner count
D            EQU   023h          ;bit count
TT           EQU   024h          ;input timer
;
Ccount       EQU   025h          ;1 ms counter var
Decade       EQU   026h          ;decade count var
Vcount       EQU   027h          ;variable counter var
VarConst     EQU   028h          ;Const for variable count
;
 ORG         00h
 BCF         STATUS,5     ;bank0
 CLRF GPIO
 MOVLW       07h
 MOVWF       CMCON        ;comparator off
 CLRF PIR1
 CLRF TICON
;
 BSF         STATUS,5     ;bank1
 CALL 3FFh         ;get calibration
 MOVWF       OSCCAL       ;set it
; do bank1 init
 CLRF OPTIONR      ;option
 CLRF PIE1
 CLRF PCON
 CLRF WPU          ;Disable weak pull ups
 CLRF IOC          ;disable interrupt on change
 CLRF VRCON
; set IO
 MOVLW       3Ch          ;5,4,3,2 in 1,0 out
 MOVWF       TRISIO
;
 BCF         STATUS,5     ;bank 0
 CLRF GPIO
;
Loop
;
;-------------------------------------------
```

```
; I input for TNodes, MoNodes
ReadI
;Find start
 MOVLW      04h          ;4, 9, 18
 MOVWF      TT           ;bit, halfword, whole word
CI
 BTFSC      GPIO,IC      ;1 look at IC
 GOTO ReadI        ;2 is on
 DECFSZ     TT           ;3
 GOTO CI           ;4 5*TT
; found start, read the word.
 CLRF D            ;start with bit 0
 CLRF TT           ;
 BCF        STATUS,0     ;
I1
 BTFSC      GPIO,IC      ;0 bit Low?
 GOTO RDIBit       ;1 no, is high, go read
 DECFSZ     TT           ;2 yes, time it
 GOTO I1           ;3 try again
 GOTO GotI         ; give up
; read bit
RDIBit
 BTFSS      GPIO,ID      ;2 yes, test bit
 GOTO ZeroI ;3 is zero
 BSF        I,7          ;4 is one, move it to I
 GOTO ComI         ;5
ZeroI
 BCF        I,7          ;4 move bit to I
 NOP                     ;5
; bit read.
ComI
 INCF D            ;7 next bit
 BTFSC      D,3          ;8 bits done?
 GOTO GotI         ;9
 BCF        STATUS,0     ;10
 RRF        I,1          ;11
 GOTO I1           ;11 Do until bits are done
GotI
;-----------------------------------------------
```

```
;
; Begin SMNode function
;
 MOVLW      moff         ;make it offset
 ADDWF      I,1          ;0 to 255
 MOVF I,W
 MOVWF      VCount       ;set up variable count
; Do servo pulse
 MOVLW      DTime       ;
 MOVWF      Decade       ;
; Servo Pulse starts /----------------------------\
 BSF        GPIO,OD            ;1 set pulse on
;
; Do 1 millisecond count for full CCW 1000 count
 MOVLW      DTime               ;2  10 set up counters
 MOVWF      Decade              ;3
BL1
 MOVLW      CTime              ;4 1 32
 MOVWF      CCount             ;5 2
MS1
 DECFSZ     CCount,1            ;1 3 .000001 seconds
 GOTO       MS1                 ;  3 MS = 2*CCount
 DECFSZ     Decade,1            ;  4
 GOTO       BL1                ;  6 BL = 5*Decade*MS
; 1000 = 2*CCount*5*Decade = 2*10*5*10 is 1.01 ms
;
; Variable time starts
; 1000 = 256*3.906 = In*3.906 (250*4 = 1000)
; Servo     counts             integer    offset
; CCW 0 counts    -128  0
; 0   500 counts  0     128
; CW  1000 counts 127   255
;
VarCount
 MOVF VCount,W    ;1
 BTFSC      STATUS,2     ;2 is VCount = 0?
 GOTO done        ;3 yes, exit
VS
 NOP                     ;1 5
 DECFSZ     VCount,1     ;2 6
 GOTO VS          ;3 7  = 4*VCount
done
 BCF        GPIO,OD            ;25 Pulse off -------
```

```
; Pulse off. Start 20 millisecond cycle - 2
; 20 milliseconds requires 200000 cycles
; Do 20 ms off cycle do 1 ms 20 times
;
 MOVLW       BigTime              ;19
 MOVWF       BigCount             ;
; 1 ms start
ML20
 MOVLW       DTime                ;
 MOVWF       Decade               ;10
BL2
 MOVLW       CTime                ;32
 MOVWF       CCount               ;makes 100
MS2
 DECFSZ      CCount,1             ;
 GOTO        MS2                  ;
 DECFSZ      Decade,1             ;
 GOTO        BL2                  ;
; 1 ms stop
 DECFSZ      BigCount,1           ;
 GOTO        ML20                 ;20*1ms
;
; End SMNode function
;
 GOTO        Loop             ;34
;
; End SMNode
 END
```

Motors are in an engineering area where you make whatever is required.

2. Motor Analogs

Nature -> Sensors -> Brain -> Motors -> **Nature**

Motor, again, is a numeric part that transforms to an analog voltage. A motor controller runs an actual motor. The type of controller must match the type of motor. Most motors require a voltage and a current source to run. Model airplane servos require a timed pulse.

Final discrimination takes place in a motor. Actions relate to the required goals of the Robot. The only general rule for motors that you can make is to have the motor do nothing if the input Hal stream is zero.

Again, you have to note that differentiation or integration may take place in the motor half that pushes nature. If this is so, it should be specified in the specifications for the motor. (You can always stick a DNode or INode in the Hal stream to correct this if need be.)

Real motors rotate. (There are linear motors as well).
Most motors run a gear train that exchanges speed for torque. There are also servos that rotate to a given angle. For Robots you can use model airplane servos and simple gear train motors for almost everything.

HalNode Cycle Times

Every HalNode might have a different cycle time. The main problem this causes is to make spreadsheet simulation impossible. A spreadsheet cannot make live HalStreams in any event. In a live Robot, the Hal stream is what it is. The Robot has no way of knowing about cycle time. Does this matter?

Suppose you have this situation:

Data Flow : Nature -> Sensors -> Brain -> Motors -> Nature
Cycle time: 1 3 2 8 1

There are 14 cycles from sensing nature to moving nature. That is, 14 changes in nature can take place while the Robot is processing data. Nature gets by with this, so you probably need not worry about it. You can always advance or delay HalStreams if you know the type.

Nature has cycles in scales of:
nanoseconds
microseconds
milliseconds
seconds
minutes
hours
days
weeks
months
years

Most Robot nodes work in microseconds. Motors work in milliseconds. Generally, you have to worry about slow inputs more than you have to worry about slow outputs.

Sensors produce data in steps. Slow inputs stretch the step interval. Amplitude will be correct, but a given value will remain as a constant until the next value is obtained. If you put the Hal stream on an x, t plot slow HalStreams stretch the time axis changing the scale.

```
Amp
4
3                                 3 3 3 3 3
2          2 2 2 2 2
1 1 1 1 1 1          1 1 1 1 1
0                                            0 0 0
0 0
0           1           2           3           4
5
  Time
```

0 0 0 0 0 1 0 0 0 0 -1 0 0 0 2 0 0 0 0 -3 0 0 0 0 is how a fast derivative would see this. Note the values are correct. We just have too many zeros in between.

When there is a huge time difference like this, the computations will be correct, but there will be spikes in the differentials. Motors will generally ignore spikes, so one may not notice any difference in the machine.

This is an area that could use more study. One could quantify time differences and the exact changes they make in the computation. Simulation of HalTrees in a computer must take care that no data changes before the entire tree cycle has completed. The Robot is doing all this in parallel so this must be taken into account with the simulation.

If need be, you can always trace the time ticks though a Robot. Simply start at the real sensors and follow each path until you reach a motor. There will be, at least, a time path for every sensor.

1. HalTrees

A combinatorial HalTree is a fully connected network of nodes, many sensors to one motor. So far you have seen algebraic statements. With HalTrees, I offer an alternate nomenclature. Two input HalNodes form HalTrees. Trees and algebra do not look the same. So I make a HalTree algebra.

A = B - C is a generic equation. The = sign says that B - C are equal to A and nothing more. I add the property of information transfer that adds causality. Now the equation A = B - C says that A = B - C and B - C sends data to A and, sometimes, B - C causes A.

The simplest tree is a single HalNode.

F = S1 - S2, two sensors to one function.

Another alternate representation when you do not need the structure is to use tree functions. This one is:

F = CTree(S1, S2, S3, S4). Use a HalTree function with a list of the sensors or inputs. Every HalTree has a solution that can be written algebraically.

When you add more sensors for more complex trees, you must also add some intermediate variables. HalStreams sweep though the tree one layer at a click of c time. The number of sensors can characterize trees. I find that there are many types of trees, full trees, sparse trees, property trees, size trees, cellular trees, identification trees, neuron trees, language trees and probably many more. A picture is best to show this. See figures 6 and 7. But I need a computational method also. Let sensors be S1 through Sn. Trees feed one motor oxx, where xx is the tree end coordinate. Trees will be named Tn.

Trees can also be shown on a grid with coordinates on the side. Then the nodes can be named from their coordinate position. Here is how this looks:

	0	1	2	3
0	s00			
1	s10	m11		
2	s20	m21	m22	
3	s30	m31	m32	o33

sxx are inputs and might be sensors. nxx are Hal nodes. The algebra of this tree is:

```
m11 = s10 + s00      ;layer 1 reads layer 0
m21 = s20 + s10
m31 = s30 + s20

m22 = m21 + m11      ;layer 2 reads layer 1
m32 = m31 + m21

o33 = m32 + m22      ;layer 3 reads layer 2
```

These are combinatorial, Pascal or full trees.

```
One input
     0    1
1    s10  o11

o11 = s10       ; Single Hal stream {s10}

Two inputs T2 = CTree(s00, s10)
     0    1
0    s00
1    s10  o11

o11 = s10 + s00     ;+ can be any node function (+,-,o,a...)

Three inputs T3 = CTree(S1, S2, S3)
     0    1    2
0    s00
1    s10  m11
2    s20  m21  o22

m11 = s10 + s00
m20 = s20 + s10

o22 = m21 + m11
```

```
For 4 inputs: o33 = CTree(s00,s10,s20,s30)
      0     1     2     3
0     s00
1     s10   m11
2     s20   m21   m22
3     s30   m31   m32   o33

m11 = s10 + s00
m21 = s20 + s10
m31 = s30 + s20

m22 = m21 + m11
m32 = m31 + m21

o33 = m32 + m22
```

The number of columns in a full tree is equal to the number of inputs.

Note that a four-sensor tree contains all the trees below it. Those above are full trees. Two input trees cannot tell the difference. They are both full, property and sparse just as the number two cannot tell addition from multiplication.

If I write T as a single equation, eliminating the memory variables, I discover something interesting.

```
o33 = m32 + m22 = m31 + m21 + m21 + m11
o33 = m31 + 2*m21 + m11
o33 = s30 + s20 + 2*s20 + 2*s10 + s10 + s00
o33 = s30 + 3*s20 + 3*s10 + s00
```

Now I have o in terms of s.

o33 = s30 + 3*s20 + 3*s10 + s00; Note the coefficients. You see the Pascal triangle under there. This is why I call them combinatorial trees. (Pascal trees?) You can just write down the T function for 5 sensors.

o44 = s40 + 4*s30 + 6*s20 + 4*s10 + s00

Given a table of Pascal's triangle, you can write down the output weighting of any number of inputs.

You can count the HalNodes and HalStreams.
Let s = number of sensors or inputs,1 2 3 4 5 …
Let N = the counting numbers, … 0 1 2 3 …
Let n = the number of nodes
Let d = the number of HalStreams

n = i(N)[s-1] - 0 ; the number of HalNodes is the (s-1)th triangular number. Of course you can use n = s!/(s-2)!*2 to compute the number of HalNodes in a full HalTree. Note how much simpler the Hal algebra statement is.

N = … 1 2 3 4 5 …
s =   0 1 2 3 4 5 …
n =   0 0 1 3 6 10 15 … ; These are the triangular numbers.

For 1 sensor, n = 0   d = 1
For 2 sensors, n = 1   d = 3
For 3 sensors, n = 3   d = 6
For 4 sensors, n = 6   d = 10
For 5 sensors, n = 10   d = 15
For 6 sensors, n = 15   d = 21
and so on.

The number of memories is n - 1 because the final output, Ts, is not called a memory.

A full tree of HalNodes retains the character of the single HalNode. In the case of CNodes, the tree has a positive side and a negative side. Feedback to the negative side oscillates. Feedback to the positive side counts, as in the single HalNode. Then the tree has its own combinatorial characteristics.

If you are not interested in the intermediate memory variables in the tree, you can express trees as functions like this:

O is the output of the tree. The inputs are the sensors S1,S2,S3,S4,… You can have a tree of any HalNode type. (Mixed HalNode type trees I will consider later.) I use a symbol to indicate HalNode type.

Symbol	HalNode	HalTree
C	CNode	CTree
P	PNode	PTree
o	ONode	OTree
a	ANode	ATree
is	ISNode	ISTree
gt	GTNode	GTTree
lt	LTNode	LTTree
was	WASNode	WASTree
wgt	WGTNode	WGTTree
wlt	WLTNode	WLTTree

These are the only nodes I will consider here. All tree functions are the same for all these, so I will use only C type below. Understand that any of the above types can be substituted. This is probably how the assembly language of Robots will develop, using tree notation.

Then I can express the function:

```
OC2 = CFTree(S1,S2) = S1 - S2
OC3 = CFTree(S1,S2,S3) = S1 - 2*S2 + S3
OC4 = CFTree(S1,S2,S3,S4) = S1 - 3*S2 +
                            3*S3 - S4
OC5 = CFTree(S1,S2,S3,S4,S5) = S1 - 4*S2 +
                            6*S3 - 4*S5
                     + S5
```

and so on.
Note that OC4 = CFTree(CFTree(S1,S2))

If you set all the sensors to 1 and use PNodes you get the series:

```
OP1 = PTree(1) = 1
OP2 = PTree(1,1) = 1 + 1 = 2
OP3 = PTree(1,1,1) = 1 + 2 + 1 = 4
OP4 = PTree(1,1,1,1) = 1 + 3 + 3 + 1 = 8
OP5 = PTree(1,1,1,1,1) = 1 + 4 + 6 + 4 + 1 = 16
OP6 = PTree(1,1,1,1,1,1) = 1 + 5 + 10 + 10 + 5 + 1 = 32
```

Let SN = number of sensors.
Let SC = sum of coefficients

$SC = 2^{(SN-1)}$

I will rewrite the coefficients so they line up better.

```
C1  C2   C3   C4   C5   C6   C7   C8   C9 = OP9
(Inputs = 1)
1                                          =   1
1 + 1                                      =   2
1 + 2 +  1                                 =   4
1 + 3 +  3 +  1                            =   8
1 + 4 +  6 +  4 +  1                       =  16
1 + 5 + 10 + 10 +  5 +  1                  =  32
1 + 6 + 15 + 20 + 15 +  6 +  1             =  64
1 + 7 + 21 + 35 + 35 + 21 +  7 + 1         = 128
1 + 8 + 28 + 56 + 70 + 56 + 28 + 8 + 1     = 256
```

And so on.

C2 is N and is the number of bits required to write the sum on the right. C3 contains the triangular numbers and the rest of the columns contain combinatorial numbers.

Each column in this display is the integral of the column before it.

C2 is i(C1) and C3 is i(C2) or in general:
C(n) = i(C(n-1)) - 0

So we have established the primary, underlying arithmetic of HalTrees. Now let's go back to CNode trees and try some other inputs.

Input the beginning of the triangular numbers, just for kicks. Here are some Pascal coefficients for your reference.

```
2: 1 - 1
3: 1 - 2 +  1
4: 1 - 3 +  3 -  1
5: 1 - 4 +  6 -  4 +  1
6: 1 - 5 + 10 - 10 +  5 -  1
7: 1 - 6 + 15 - 20 + 15 -  6 +  1
8: 1 - 7 + 21 - 35 + 35 - 21 +  7 - 1
9: 1 - 8 + 28 - 56 + 70 - 56 + 28 - 8 + 1
```

```
OCn = CTree(S1,S2,S3,S4,S5,…n)
OC2 = CTree(1,3) = 1*1-3*1 = -2
OC3 = CTree(1,3,6) = 1*1 - 3*2 + 6*1 = 1
OC4 = CTree(1,3,6,10) = 1*1 - 3*3 + 6*3 - 10*1 = 0
OC5 = CTree(1,3,6,10,15) =1*1 -3*4 + 6*6 - 10*4 + 15*1 = 0
…
```

```
OC4 = CTree(1,2,2,1) = 1*1-2*3+2*3-1*1 =   0
OC4 = CTree(1,1,1,1) = 1*1-1*3+1*3-1*1 =   0
OC4 = CTree(1,3,1,3) = 1*1-3*3+1*3-3*1 =  -8
OC4 = CTree(1,4,1,4) = 1*1-4*3+1*3-4*1 = -12
OC4 = CTree(4,1,4,1) = 4*1-1*3+4*3-1*1 =  12
OC4 = CTree(3,1,4,1) = 3*1-1*3+4*3-1*1 =   6
```

This is what a full HalTree looks like in a spreadsheet:

```
     Input mem1 mem2 Output
     A     B    C    D
Row1 s1
           m11
Row2 s2         m21
           m12       o33
Row3 s3         m22
           m13
Row4 s4
```

```
The equations are:
m11 = S2 - s1
m12 = S3 - s2
m13 = S4 - s3

m21 = m12 - m11 ;m2x = d(m1x)
m22 = m13 - m12

o33 = m22 - m21 ;o33 = d(m2x)
```

You can write every full tree in this format, which shows some of its relationships. The numbers are: Column and row. This tree is made of CNodes. This is also a spreadsheet format.

In	**c1**	**c2**	**c3**	**c4**
s11				
	m21			
s12		m31		
	m22		m41	
s13		m32		OC4
	m23		m42	
s14		m33		
	m24			
s15				

With CNodes, m2x = d(s1x) and m3x = d(m2x) and so on.

Let's put in some numbers. First N.

In	c1	c2	c3	c4
1				
	1			
2		0		
	1		0	
3		0		0
	1		0	
4		0		
	1			
5				

Now doubling numbers:

In	c1	c2	c3	c4
1				
	1			
2		1		
	2		1	
4		2		1
	4		2	
8		4		
	8			
16				

Now tripling numbers:

In	c1	c2	c3	c4
1				
	2			
3		4		
	6		8	
9		12		16
	18		24	
27		36		
	54			
81				

Note that all the diagonal numbers are doubling numbers.

Let's write down another tree with the differences in the rows from column to column.

In	c1	c2	c3	c4	
1					
	2				;3 - 2
3		4			
	6		8		;9 - 6
9		12		16	;27 - 18
	18		24		
27		36			
	54				;81 - 54
81					

How is that for being fractal?

How about putting some combinatorial numbers in a CTree like this:

In	**c1**	**c2**	**c3**	**c4**	**c5**
1					
	5				
6		10			
	15		10		
21		20		5	
	35		15		1
56		35		6	
	70		21		
126		56			
	126				
252					

Put the diagonal in a PTree.

In	**c1**	**c2**	**c3**	**c4**	**c5**
1					
	6				
5		21			
	15		56		
10		35		126	
	20		70		252
10		35		126	
	15		56		
5		21			
	6				
1					

And there is a relation between combinatorial numbers and Pascal tree numbers, all done mechanically.

Detecting objects with CNode trees. An object is a self similar patch in a field. Set up a column of sensors of the kind you need to detect these objects.

A	B	C	D	E
S1				
	d(A1)			
S2		d2(A1)		
	d(A2)		d3(A1)	
S3		d2(A2)		d4(A1)
	d(A3)		d3(A2)	
S4		d2(A3)		
	d(A4)			
S5				

If S1 = S2 then d(A1) = 0
If S1 = S2 = S3 then d(A1) = d(A2) = d2(A1) = 0
If S1 = S2 = S3 = S4 then d(A1) to d3(A2) = 0
If all sensors are equal, the entire tree is 0.

To detect the length of the object, set up a code for each. Length1 = d(A1) z 1 ; if d(A1) = 0 then Length1 = 1

Length2 = sum(d(A1):d2(A2) z 2 ; and so on for all the sensors. You will see this applied in both eyes and ears later on.

A tree of ISNodes directly pulls objects from a tree.

Here is a tree of ISNodes

```
s1
     is1
s2        is21
     is2       is31
s3        is22
     is3
s4
```

If s1 is s2 then is1 will be s1
If s2 is s3 then is2 = s2
If s3 is s4 then is3 = s3
If is1 is is2 then is21 = is1
If is2 is is3 then is22 = is2
If is21 is is22 then is3 = is21

So here, if there are no objects, there are all zeroes. If there are objects, we get their intensity. Size is related to isxx level. isx objects are the smallest. is2x objects are next size up and is31 is largest. Note that ISNodes compare the equality of all its inputs at the same time. is31 has a value only when s1 = s2 = s3 = s4.

The main peculiarity of ISNode trees are that zero valued objects all return 1. All values other than equality are seen as zeroes. If you are detecting other qualities, use another tree in addition to the ISNode tree.

Trees can also be written in set notation, leaving off the tree specification.

This tree = {this variable, that variable, a, b, c } implying they will be expanded later.

There is of course a null tree.

Null tree = {}

2. Sparse trees

Again, use sensors S1 to Sn.

A two input tree:

T2 = S1 o S2

Three input sparse tree:

m1 = S1 o S2
T3 = m1 o S3

Four inputs:

m1 = S1 o S2
m2 = S3 o S4
T4 = m1 o m2

Again, eliminating the memory variables, you obtain:
T = S1 o S2 o S3 o S4 ; All the coefficients are 1.

The number of nodes required is one less than the number of inputs.

ONodes and ANodes can use sparse HalTrees all the time, since they work exactly the same in either.

Since all the coefficients of sparse trees are 1, you can use them where no center bias or weighting is required.
The function CSTree(S1,S2,S3,S4) is S1 - S2 + S3 - S4

Sparse trees are good to use when you are preserving direction. Lets build a sparse direction tree.

Direction = d1 - d2
 d1 = SLL o SLR

d2 = SRL o SRR

Note we had to use a mixed tree to properly get the direction.
Also Direction = CTree(OTree(SLL,SLR) - OTree(SRL,SRR)).

Full and Sparse Trees

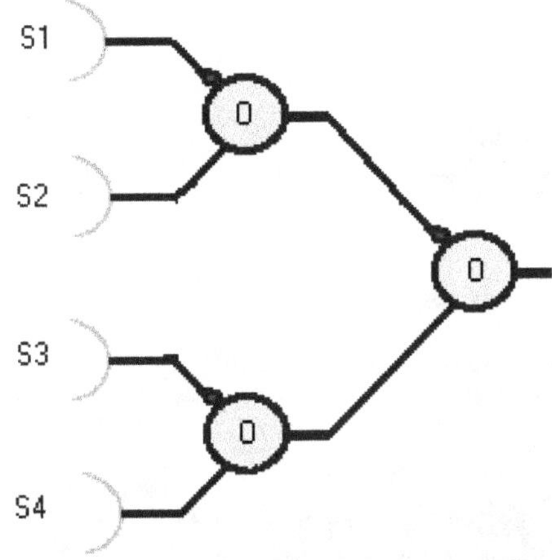

Sparse OTree

O = S1 o S2 o S3 o S4

A sparse ONode tree

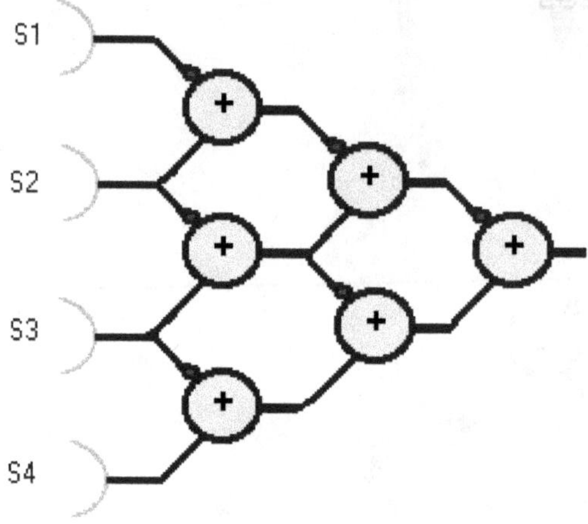

O = S1 + 3*S2 + 3*S3 + S4

A Full PNode Tree

Figure 9 Trees

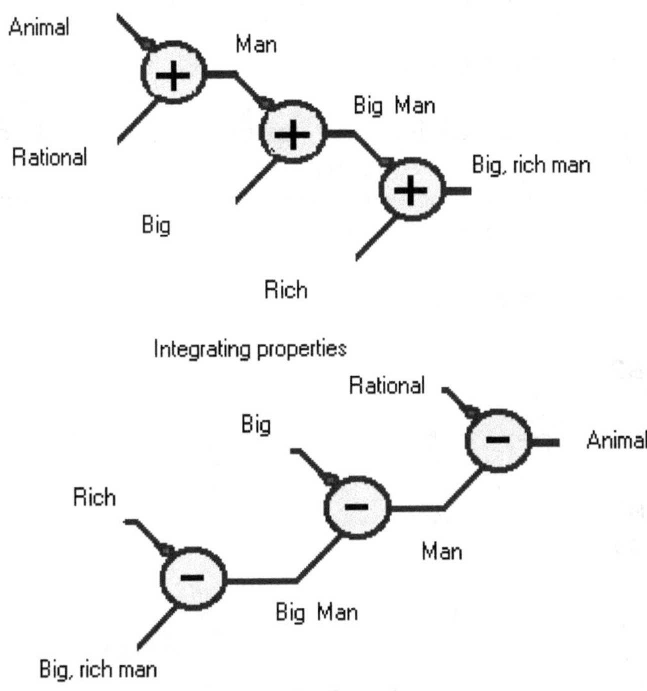

Figure 10 Property Trees

2. Property Trees

How trees connect to language. The sensor row of the tree carries the most complete description of the tree concept. Each property tree is a concept, a function and a motor. As a concept, as you go down the tree, collecting sensors into trees the concept becomes more and more abstract. That is, as you go up the tree from the final motor, you must add more description to the variable names. If the motor name is X then up the tree will be XL and

XR and from XL up will be XLU and XLD and from XR will be XRU and XRD. Going up the tree is integration and you are adding variables. Going down the tree is differentiation and you are removing variables or properties.

Property Tree functions:

A property tree is the outer diagonal of a regular full tree. Again, let us have sensors of s1 to sn and trees of p1 to pn. Property trees are of the form:

Two input property trees

P1 = s1 + s2

Three input property trees

P1 = s1 + s2
P2 = p1 + s3

Four input property trees

P1 = s1 + s2
P2 = p1 + s3
P3 = p2 + s4

Five input property trees

p1 = s1 + s2
p2 = p1 + s3
p3 = p2 + s4
p4 = p3 + s5

And so on. Property trees are made of property trees.

The reason I call these property trees is shown by a change in variable name.

Integration of a concept:

man = rational + animal
big man = man + big
rich big man = big man + rich

and so on.

Also, differentiation of a concept:

big man = rich big man - rich
man = big man - big
animal = man - rational

And so on. These property trees are what they are. There is no tree notation, i.e. no solution from eliminating variables. Here it is the variables we want.

2. Trees with mixed HalNode types

As you have seen, trees of the same type compute combinatorial numbers. OT = CTree(a, b, c, d) If you cycle through the values of {a, b, c, d] you get zeroes for all equal or linear values but you lose direction. The tree is symmetric and weighted toward the center. The last HalNode that feeds the motor always gives direction and if you make that a CNode, you retain direction if the two sides of the HalNode are collected for it. For example:

let OT = Left - right;
Then if Left = a + b
and Right = c + d

Then you know which side is bigger, so you know direction.
From arithmetic, you know that the sum of the differences equals the difference of the sums. So you get exactly the same result if OT = Left + Right
and Left = a - b
and Right = c - d

This also works, getting values instead of aggregates:
OT = Left - Right
Left = a o b
Right = c o d

With a CNode at the tree end, its two sides can be made up of any structure needed. In general, the CNode weighs the right and left or chooses the right or left. The CNode does not care what feeds it.

2. The permutations of connecting sensors to trees

Sensors connect to motors, always. Given a bunch of sensors and a HalTree, how many ways can you connect the sensors to the HalTree?

Number the sensors by number. Here is a picture. S is the sensor picture, c1 is the count of ones, c2 the count of twos, c6 the count of sixes and connections is the total count of possible connections.

S	c1	c2	c6	connections	Comments
1	1	1		1	1 sensor
12	1				
21	2	2		2	2 sensors
123	1				
132	2	1			
213	3				
231	4	2			
312	5				
321	6	3	1	6	3 sensors
1234	1				
1243	2	1			
1324	3				
1342	4	2			
1423	5				
1432	6	3	1		
2134	7				
2143	8	4			
2314	9				
2341	10	5			
2413	11				
2431	12	6	2		
3124	13				
3142	14	7			
3214	15				
3241	16	8			
3412	17				
3421	18	9	3		
4123	19				
4132	20	10			
4213	21				
4231	22	11			
4312	23				
4321	24	12	4	24	4 sensors

No. Sensors	M1 tree	pos. connections
1	1	1
2	1	2
3	1	6
4	1	24
5	1	120
6	1	720

The number of ways you can connect n sensors to a tree of n virtual motors is n! (n factorial is 1*2*3*4...*n). This is the permutation of n things taken n at a time. This also means if you connect n sensors at random you will get one of n! different behaviors.

2. The Combinatorials of HalTree Inputs

$C = b^I$ where b is the number base of the tree and I is the number of inputs. This is how many different inputs can be input into the tree. To see how this was developed, imagine that you must write down every possible input to a HalTree or neuron of size x. Treat every sensor output as a digit of base b. Write down the digit names. Any order will do since you are interested in total input possibilities, so digit order will not matter. Then start at zero and count upward by one. This will guarantee every code. It is also mostly impossible to do except for trivial examples.

Given a tree of size 4, write down the sensors as digits. Let the base be 2 for this exercise. You might want to record the output of the tree.

d1	**d2**	**d3**	**d4**	**Count**
0	0	0	0	0
0	0	0	1	1
0	0	1	0	2
0	0	1	1	3
0	1	0	0	4
0	1	0	1	5
0	1	1	0	6
0	1	1	1	7
1	0	0	0	8
1	0	0	1	9
1	0	1	0	10
1	0	1	1	11
1	1	0	0	12
1	1	0	1	13
1	1	1	0	14
1	1	1	1	15

C = 2^4 = 16

Note that you can adjust both base and number of digits to obtain any state count. For example C1 = 4^2 = 16.

Just recently I saw a count of human brain connections. It was 10^21 digits. We do not know the number base of neurons since no one has thought about it until now. If the number base is b then the state number of the human brain is b^(10^21) which blows up my calculator.

2. Language Parse Trees

All languages have subject S, object O and verb V as sentence SS structures in all languages. A general parse tree is SS = S o V o O where S O and V can be tree structures as well.

I do not know the size of the language parse tree. There can be several in parallel.

Language comes in to the listener as a serial stream. That is converted into a parse tree by feeding the sentence through a set of serially connected nodes which then feed the parse tree. So the tree always has data from the first input to the end.

Suppose the input is: "The happy boy eats ice cream".

"The" is first thing in the tree. Then
"The happy". Then
"The happy boy". Then
"The happy boy eats". Then
"The happy boy eats ice". and finally
"The happy boy eats ice cream".

To do computation on language, it must first be converted into numbers. I am still working on how to do that. What this means is that every SS is a number that can be combined with other SS numbers to any extent. All of these language parts are properties, whose sums become concepts.

The language tree is the one that must also work in reverse. We must go from concept to sentence as well as sentence to concept. We have: sound goes to number goes to identification goes to concepts goes to memory. All the elements here are Hal trees. The trees do not work in reverse, but we have memory of objects and concepts that can be combined into new trees and then run through parallel to serial mechanism to produce speech that is the exact reverse of the input in form.

NP = (det)+ A* + N1 + VP + NP2
As a two input tree, we need temporary variables that I will call Tx where x is a digit value.

T1 = (det) + A1 ; or zero
T2 = A2 + A3 ; or zero
T3 = A4 + N1

T11 = T1 + T2
NP = T3 + T11

VP = V - NotV

T4 = A5 + A6 ;or zero
NP2 = T4 + N2

T5 = NP + VP
S1 = NP2 + T5

The tree can be made as large as the largest sentence if you want. Then it will have lots of empty spaces that will do no harm at all. S will have a number from the beginning of the sentence sound to the end. All the sounds will become codes that ultimately will have meaning in the sense of identification with sound and other sensors.

Sentences can be combined as are any other Hal trees. Trees designed for questions can be made with slight change in the order of connection to the tree. Go back to S, O, V and SS. SS = S + V + O ; for statements. Bob is hungry.
SQ = V + S + O ; for questions. Is Bob hungry?

Hungry = hunger GT hungerlevel
Ans = Bob is Hungry ;Hungry = hunger - hungerlevel or 0

2. Feedback

While there is some memory in tree networks, permanent memory is in feedback loops and special structures. Here you leave the computer and go into uncharted territory. Tree networks can be run on spreadsheets, but feedback loops break computers.

Natural feedback from actions is not direct. Generally, there will be some divisor of the action and a time delay. For the general HalNode:

how = what - where ; you usually provide a sensor on **where** that relates the action from **how**. This provides negative feedback so the process tends to center, with **how** = 0.

how = what - where

If you reverse **what** and **where** so you have:

how = where - what

how = where - what ; then you will tend to lock up at some maximum or minimum **how**.

Feedback is extremely context sensitive. It matters greatly how the motor and sensors are arranged. If you are controlling some action, you must arrange the motor and sensors so that a zero from the HalNode indicates the stopping point. For example, say you are controlling the speed of an engine. You measure the speed and send it to the R input of a CNode. You have a dial, marked as speed, (RPM) that produces a Hal stream that you connect to the L input. You want to obtain this RPM. The O output of the CNode is connected to the motor that in turn is connected to the throttle. When the motor is still, the throttle does not move. When the motor turns, the throttle moves so that RPM is increased with positive rotation and decreased with negative rotation.

Now, after all this, you have a little servo. You can dial in an RPM and the engine will follow. The reason for the extra motor for the throttle is that the output of the CNode is the change in RPM needed. The change is used to set the throttle position, so the throttle integrates the output of the motor. The position of the throttle produces a fixed RPM from the engine, changing position to speed. That RPM is compared to the RPM you have dialed in, and the position of the throttle is moved until the two RPM measurements are equal, no matter what.

With feedback, you have to pay attention to units. You may have to integrate or differentiate a Hal stream to make the units match. Sometimes, as in our example, the hardware itself performs the unit change. Nature is full of integrators and differentiators. Fortunately, most of them are simple changes of position to velocity and back.

2. Manipulating Time and Offset in HalStreams

The Hal stream passing through any Hal-Node has a present time, a past time and a future time. It takes a time of c to shift one to the other through the HalNode. There is another way to shift time in the Hal stream as I have noted previously. Simply adding or subtracting a lower degree Hal stream can shift some Hal stream types in time, forward or backward.

Constant HalStreams cannot be shifted, since they are the same at all times. Adding or subtracting a constant can offset them.

Polynomials can be shifted or offset. The rule for time shifting a polynomial is to add or subtract its derivative. Anything else will simply be an offset.

The polynomial of degree 1 (N) cannot be offset. Adding a constant is adding a derivative and anything added or subtracted is a shift in time. In order to shift a Hal stream in time you must know its derivative. If you have the derivative Hal stream, you know how to be anywhere in time on the Hal stream created from the derivative. By adding or subtracting the derivative to the polynomial Hal stream, you shift it upward or backward in relative time. Only the derivative will do this. If the Hal stream has no derivative that is ultimately a constant, then the Hal stream is not a polynomial and what you are adding or subtracting is an offset.

Some examples:

A constant is the same everywhere. Its derivative is zero.

N = {0 1 2 3 4 5 6 …} has a derivative of one.

Anything you add or subtract from an N Hal stream shifts it in time. N = {0 1 2 3 4 5 6 …}

+ {1 1 1 1 1 1 1 …}

= {1 2 3 4 5 6 7 …} ; we shift forward 1 click.

2N = {0 2 4 6 8 10 …}
+2 {2 2 2 2 2 2 …}
= {2 4 6 8 10 12 …} ; We shift up 1 click.

2N = {0 2 4 6 8 10 ...}
-2 {2 2 2 2 2 2 ...}
= {-2 0 2 4 6 8 ...}

For any kN we use k to shift 1 click. Use nkN to shift n clicks.

The same applies to higher degree polynomials, but now the derivatives are not constant. To properly shift a higher degree polynomial in time you must start adding derivatives at the proper point so the derivatives line up with the polynomial.

For any Hal stream S
S1 = S - d(S) ; shifts down 1
S2 = S1 - d(S1) ; S shifted 2
SP1 = S2 + d(S1) ; S2 shifted back 1

t is time.

t	**S**	**d(S)**	**S1**	**d(S1)**	**S2**	**SP1**
0	1	1	0	0	0	0
1	2	1	1	1	0	1
2	4	2	2	1	1	2
3	8	4	4	2	2	4
4	9	1	8	4	4	8
5	11	2	9	1	8	9
6	10	-1	11	2	9	11

1. Hal algebra as a Coding Language

Hal algebra can be treated as a programming language to code Robots.

This language is the machine code for Robots. That means that each line is a single HalNode and is the lowest level you can go, both in coding and physically.

The language is fully delimited so you can use long variable names with spaces if you desire. Semi colons are used to delimit comments. The code list should be computer readable since later on they will be in a development system that will check connections, provide a parts list, run simulations and all the things a development system should do. It will be called: Hal Developer. Hal Developer can now read text and rich text. (Note Pad and Word Pad.)

To code a Robot you must change your point of view and continually work at keeping it changed. You are not writing instructions to a machine here. You are writing instructions to build a machine that takes its instructions from nature. Don't tell the Robot what to do. Give it goals and actions to accomplish and the structure to read nature. You are its DNA. Your algebra is the Robot's proteins. (It took me 35 years to make this change. You have an advantage since I have already done it.)

2. The Coding Rule

The Hal algebra machine coding rule is simple.

1. Write a single HalNode equation on each line. If there are comments about the HalNode, write a ; and then your comment. For example:

Acting = action - inaction ; is a sample CNode equation. Generally MotorAction = MotorGo - MotorStop ; with data flow from sensor to motor. However, this is an algebra and it is also true that MotorGo = MotorAction + MotorStop and so on. Note there are no rules of sequence except across the equal sign. Acting is the consequence of action and inaction. The only problem this rule will cause is that you will have to name all the variables when building HalTrees.

Hal stream flow is across the equal sign. As shown, that is right to left. Here is a picture, with time (4 ticks) going down the page:

Time	**Acting =**	**action -**	**inaction**
0	x	2	1
1	1	3	2
2	1	4	3
3	1	x	x

Acting is one time tick away from action and inaction, or more generally, O is one time tick away from I and R, a fact you can usually ignore.

It makes absolutely no difference in which order you write the separate equations. You are free of the constraints of computer languages. There are no address labels in Hal algebra code. You can group code into groups of your choice, in any presentation order you prefer.

Doing = Do - Don't ;and
Done = Doing z DoneCode ; are the same as

Done = Doing z DoneCode ; then
Doing = Do - Don't ; are the same since all nodes are active all the time. This actually helps in coding since you can always assume data is available when you ask for it.

Variable names can be chosen in any style:

1. as hardware. **Rudder = sensorL - sensorR**
2. as actions. **doing = do - don't** ; like commands

   direction = WhatsLeft - whatsRight ; like information
3. as both.

   RudderTurning = RudderTurn - RudderNot-Turn

The variables names you choose are for you and your readers, since, finally we can pass around instructions for building Robots. The Robot does not generally know or need to know these names.

In a three dimensional world you may want to encode direction, left, right, forward, back, up and down. In addition you may need to encode which body part is acting. I have developed a convention of naming variables with body parts in front, then action, then direction. Make a two character code for body parts, a one character code for direction and use action in the middle. For example, if your Robot has a knee that bends the equation could be: **knBendingL = knBendL - knNotBendL**

knBendL = {HalTree to bend left knee}

knNotBendL = {HalTree to not bend left knee}

A Robot, in nature, needs to determine properties of objects and finally, objects that are in nature. Properties of objects are direction, size, color, sound, coming, going, and so on. Concept formation is the accumulation of object properties in an additive fashion.

A Robot, in nature, needs to move itself and rearrange nature. Motor actions are turning, walking, sitting, standing, drinking, breathing, peeing, reaching, clasping, and so on. You can use yourself for examples. Later on the compiler may make all the action verbs for you.

Internally, a Robot needs to have some goals to accomplish. Again, use yourself as an example. All goals will have do and don't do trees just like any other motor. Rules are like "don't bump into objects", "Conserve energy", or anything you can describe with Hal algebra.

In design, start with establishing the real motors. When the motors have been established, you can name the actions for them. Generally a motor is doing something. Then you connect a CNode to each motor and establish the HalTrees that feed it, all the do and don't HalTrees, ending at real sensors.

1. List all real motors and sensors.
2. List all actions of the motors.
3. write and draw the code from motor out to sensor.

3a. Collect the HalStreams from sensors to motor.

There are three types of trees, full or Pascal trees, sparse trees and property trees. There are also mixtures of these. The situation is:

MotorAction = AllPlus - AllMinus ; MotorAction is a single Hal stream (an axon). AllPlus and AllMinus are trees of HalNodes. Design then is defining AllPlus and AllMinus until you reach a real sensor. It helps that all motors are independent, even if they share sensors with another motor, so if you get the motor to do the action you want then it will do the same in concert with all the other motors. So you can focus on each motor or you can assign a motor to each member of your design group. You can experiment, build and tear down by simply plugging, and unplugging cable plugs into headers. This maps perfectly to your code.

Command HalTrees do not have to be symmetrical. CTrees terminated with a PNode give the same result from the rules of arithmetic.(Difference of a sum = sum of a difference.) There is no practical limit on the size of command HalTrees, but they are generally not large.

There are two ways to collect data from sensors in command HalTrees. If you want a cumulative aggregate where every sensor adds its contribution, where all sensors shout as a crowd and it is crowd noise you want, then make the HalTree of PNodes.

If you want to choose the loudest, or quietest, sensor, to pick one out of the crowd, use ONodes or ANodes to build the HalTree. Since HalTrees are made of HalTrees, mix and match to suit the situation.

If you want to detect equality use ISNodes. ISNodes will detect the equality time of any number of sensors. If several conditions have to be equal before you can do something, use ISNodes. (Use is, gt, lt for equal greater than or less than conditions.)

2. Direction

The first thing a Robot would like to know is the direction it should steer (to or from). When it finds the direction it sends it to the steering motor tree as one of the motors instructions.

A CNode will always give you direction. The sensors should be spaced apart. Only two sensors are needed for direction or you can use two HalTrees. As variables their HalStreams will carry location in space of the sensors. Then direction is:
HDirection = sLeft - sRight ; You can establish a convention of minus being left or vice versa. What this means is you put HDirection on the appropriate side of the motor's tree. Also to account for is whether this sensed thing is to follow or flee. This transfers the convention to the Robot.

Direction = Left - Right

2. Collection

Collecting information is another simple task with Hal algebra. Collecting is building a tree from the sensors inward to a collection point. Moving from the sensors to the collection point removes description and makes the data more abstract and general.

The information collected is generally from sensors or designated HalStreams. You might collect touch sensors from fingers to hand to side to general being touched. What you do with the collected information depends on requirements. You could have the Robot move and so on.

Remember, CNodes differentiate s. PNodes aggregate s. ONodes pick the loudest s. ANodes pick the quietest s.

Collection = AllLeft + AllRight
AllLeft = {HalTree on left side}
AllRight = {HalTree on right side}

Other things to collect are all Doing things and Done things and Done (some time period).

2. Object detection

A Robot in nature needs to be able to detect objects around it and their properties. General properties of visual objects are size, shape, color, how moving and so on. That there is an object is contained in C1 of the HalTree. If any HalNode in C1 is zero, that means the two sensors feeding it are equal, defining object. You have to tap into the HalTree to detect the zero. Using the other detection nodes allows you to determine shadings with the objects. Detecting plus in C1 is shading away. Detecting minus in C1 is shading to.

ObjectFound = ds4 z foundCode ; if you are looking at s3 and s4.
UpShadeR = ds3 g UpShadeCodeR
UpShadeL = ds5 g UpShadeCodeL
DownShadeR = ds3 l DownShadeCodeR
DownShadeL = ds5 l DownShadeCodeL

You can also use detection nodes directly now.
ObjectFound = s3 is s4 ;eliminate the CNodes
UpShadeR = s3 gt s4
DownShadeR = s3 lt s4
UpShadeL = s4 gt s5
DownShadeL = s4 lt s5

You can, of course, make a HalTree of objects found, which would be adding another level of HalTree, which you can do to any degree of levels you need in the brain or Robot you are building.

2. Object Location

Object location is finding the direction of an object, so it means applying object detection at least at two points to determine where. Possibilities are an object is left or right or both or there are two objects. Anyhow, we make a detection HalTree from the sensor HalTree.

ObjectLeft = ds2 z s1 ;give the actual sensor value
ObjectRight = ds6 z s5 ;for the appropriate sensor

ObjectLocation = ObjectLeft - ObjectRight

isObj = ObjectLeft o ObjectRight

Om1 = isObj is ObjectLeft
ObjectFound = Om1 is ObjectRight

2. Object Size

Size, actually length here, is found buy measuring how many sensors are covered by the same values at this location. We have already detected the smallest object when we were finding objects. That was obj1 = dsx z 1 where dsx is any sensor we choose.

To determine if more than two sensors are covered we have to go to another row in the HalTree. (Note, if the all the sensors have the same value, the entire tree is zero, so we would detect the entire tree by looking at the last output, insuring that it really is a zero HalTree by adding up all the columns or the diagonal.

```
Object1 = dsx z 1
m1 = dsx + d2sx
Object2 = m1 z 2  ;Object2 = (dsx+d2sx) z 2
m11 = dsx + d2sx
m12 = m11 + d3sx
Object3 = m12 z 3   ;Object3 = (dsx+d2sx+d3sx)
z 3
```

and so on to 255 object lengths.

If you are finding object size in more than one location, and you should be, then you will have to qualify the variables by including location in their names.

By this time you are collecting object and property HalTrees, so your Robot can locate where the largest objects are and can send that to a command HalTree.

2. Object Motion

A HalTree set up for detection also computes relative motion. If a second row value is zero the sensors are equal. If a second row value is positive, the sensor amplitude is rising, while if it is negative, the value is falling. To detect positive and negative I have to complete the detection HalNodes with G and L nodes. Then we can detect zero, plus and minus, which, in vision gives us objects and whether their environment is coming toward us or going away from us. In vision, or generally, the full HalTree of CNodes and the detection trees give the Robot a constant picture of what is out there. The incoming detection trees now go to make up figures in the figure/ground scene. All objects that move together are figures.

Coming = ds5 l s5 ; if ds5 is negative, Coming = s5

Going = ds5 g s5 ; if ds5 is positive, Going = s5

2. Serial to Parallel

Sometimes you only have a single Hal stream to work with, but you would like to make it into a HalTree for detection and so forth. Here is a neat way I found when working with ears. It allows you to adjust the amplitude of the Hal stream before you convert it to a HalTree.

Given the single Hal stream S, convert it to parallel. Run S through a string of PNodes.

```
s1 = S + volume      ;1 2 3 4 5 6
s2 = s1 + volume     ;1 2 3 4 5
s3 = s2 + volume     ;1 2 3 4
s4 = s3 + volume     ;1 2 3
s5 = s4 + volume     ;1 2
s6 = s5 + volume     ;1
```

Now s1, s2, s3, s4, s5, s6 can be combined in any HalTree. Set volume plus to add volume, minus to reduce volume. There is a little time delay when the sx values get refreshed, so you might or might not take this into account.

S -> s1 -> s2 -> s3 -> s4 -> s5 -> s6. All the values of S travel through S1 through S6. This is all right. This S is moving past a window. The size of the window depends on how many PNodes are used. The HalTree made of s1 - s6 can be ONodes for loudness in this window and CNodes for change in this window.

2. Sequential Actions

Quite often a motor action must wait for another motor action to complete before it can start. This has a general solution for servo type motors:

Action1 = d(Action0) z Act1
Action2 = d(Action1) z Act2 ; and so on.

Using d(action) does not ask where it is, but has it stopped? It is not using feedback from the motor position, but from the motor's instruction. You could use position or motion sensors on the moving part with better results.

2. Past, Present and Future

Immediate memory is inherent in the language. If a HalNode is Doing something, like:
Doing = Do - Don't ; Then
Done = Doing z Do ; until we get memory. Done is Doing in the past.

Anticipation of future values can be derived from differentials, since they measure change. If, for example, if a Hal stream value is rising steadily, one can anticipate it will have a greater value in the future.
Future = d(present). With the integral, one can create future values. N = i(1)-1 creates all N in the future. d(N) tells us how to anticipate.

2. Memory and Recall

How memory works is still an unsolved problem. We know all about recording data but not much about memory and recall. What little we do know is not of much help to robot builders. We know that memory is memory of something. So we must speak of memory of objects, events, conditions or whatever. The mechanism we have known before the computer. A signal is turned into a sign. X becomes M, which remains regardless of X.

When I developed Hal algebra and its hardware I started with the CNode, ONode and ANode set. You can build all active parts with those tools, just as you can build any logic statement with OR and NOT or AND and NOT. However, the more tools the better, as shown by the huge number of logic gates on the market. Hal nodes are microcontrollers (MC) with one or two inputs and one output. Internally, the inputs are the variables L and R. The output is Out. Additionally, there are the variables DI and M that will be used in some nodes.

Soon the Hal nodes began to separate into classes. The first are the arithmetic nodes that make Hal trees. They are: Arith = {c, p, o, a, *, /}
These nodes can be shown as equations in L,R and O.
They are: Out = L f R ; where f is one of the Arith operators. They do this code:

```
BEGIN Arith
Loop
 Read L
 Read R
 Do Out = L f R
 Write O
 GOTO Loop
END Arith
```

These are active all the time and continuously. I also needed nodes that were inactive until something happened. These I called logic nodes. They are:
Logic = {is, isgt, islt}
Only the primitive one bit operators are made into nodes.

These can be expressed as equations also.
Out = L cond R ; where cond = an operator in Logic. For example:
Out = L is R ; for is node

The code is:

```
BEGIN Logic
Loop
 Read L
 Read R
 If L cond R then Out = L else Out = 0
 Write Out
 GOTO Loop
END Logic
```

IS detects vertical or horizontal events like ... 5 5 5 5 5 5.... All inputs must be equal before anything but 0 is output. GT detects falling events like ... 5 4 3 2 1 .... Each input must be larger than any other for every input. LT detects rising events like ... 1 2 3 4 5 .... Each input must be smaller than any other for every input. All these emit either L-R or 0.

All these nodes work in the present. None have any memory. However, from IS, it is easy to go to WAS. The past tense of the logic nodes makes sense mechanically as well as linguistically.

We have: WLogic = {weq, wgt, wlt} which matches the logic nodes.

To make was nodes requires a slight change in program. Now we need M for memory. The code is like:

```
BEGIN WNode
 M = 0
Loop
 Read L
 Read R
 If L cond R then M = L
 Out = M
 Write Out
 GOTO Loop
END WNode
```

cond = {=, >, <} = {E, G, L}

Was nodes do not decay. They are reset only with zero data conditions. They do, however, change with each change in conditions, so they will numerically match current is nodes at all times.

WEQ remembers horizontal or vertical lines. All inputs are equal like ...5 5 5 5 5 5... WGT remembers falling events like ... 5 4 3 2 1. WLT remembers rising events like ... 1 2 3 4 5 ....

All the above are Hal tree nodes. That is they create and work in Hal trees. I suggest that memory, or was nodes be parallel to current trees. That is, if you have a see tree, then have a seen tree with the same inputs. Then you can compare what you have now with the past.

A tree of logic nodes does nothing to the tree except pass data through. The output of the tree is the logical truth of all the tree inputs. Here is an example of a 4 input tree with inputs A, B, C and D. Output is Out. For each logic tree:

<u>1 2 3</u>
A
B
C N1
D N2 Out ;All Logic trees can be sparse trees.

N1, N2 and Out are Hal nodes. A B C D are sensors.

EQ: Out = A = B = C = D or 0
GT: Out = A > B > C > D or 0
LT: Out = A < B < C < D or 0
The numeric value that comes out of the tree is A
or A - B or 0.

Memory trees compute the same output but remembers the last time the condition occurred.

WE: Out = A = B = C = D or M ; where M is A or past A.
WG: Out = A > B > C > D or M
LT: Out = A < B < C < D or M

The difference between present time and past time is Out is present and M is past. In WE for example when WE = A, M is set to A, so if you have present and past looking at the same data, they will be equal.

In addition, there is need to examine a single stream of data and make decisions and do switching. These nodes are switches. The conditions one can detect from a single stream of data are its relation to zero. That is =, >, < being exactly 3 conditions which we can call z, g and l.

So switches are: switch = {z, g, l}

All of these nodes detect one of these conditions on the Hal stream and switch a new Hal stream into the flow if the condition is met. These also can be expressed as equations.

Out = I cond R ; where cond is in switch. For example:

Out = I z R

As code:

```
BEGIN switch
Loop
 Read I
 Read R
 If I cond 0 then Out = R else Out = 0
 Write Out
 GOTO Loop
END switch
```

These nodes do not make trees. They are pure switches.
The cond of a single data stream is 0, + or - or Z, G and L.
Cond = {Z, G, L}
So we have Z, G and L nodes.

Output of the switch nodes is the data at R or 0.

I	E	G	L
0	R	0	0
1	0	R	0
-1	0	0	R

There are was nodes for switches as well.

They are WZ, WG and WL

I	WZ	WG	WL
0	R	M	M
1	M	R	M
-1	M	M	R

We must have at least a base 3 number, an integer, to make these switches all work.

With a single Hal stream you can also differentiate it with dZ, dG and dL conditions. The code for these is like:

```
BEGIN DSwitch
 OldI = 0
Loop
 Read I
 Read R
 DI = I - OldI
 IF DI cond 0 then Out = R else Out = 0
 Write Out
 OldI = I
 GOTO Loop
END DSwitch
```

With memory, the MDSwitch is:

```
BEGIN MDSwitch
 OldI = 0
Loop
 Read I
 Read R
 DI = I - OldI
 IF DI cond 0 then M = R
 Out = M
 Write Out
 OldI = I
 GOTO Loop
END MDSwitch
```

These remember the conditions {=,>,<} or {EQ,GT,LT} on Hal trees or Hal streams. Logic nodes detect these conditions. WLogic nodes detect and remember these conditions. By mixing nodes you can generate all the 16 logic conditions. For example XOR = GT + LT.

Yet another form of memory is when a variable is internally changed and remembered. The form of these is:
Out = Out f I ;where f is {+,-,*,/} Here is how the TNode Plus works:

```
BEGIN Plus
 Out = 0
 OldI = 0
Loop
 Read I
 If OldI <> I Then Out = Out + I
 Write Out
 OldI = I
 GOTO Loop
END Plus
```

Out is memory here.

As you can see, there is plenty of work left to do here. This is just the beginning. However, working with WLogic will help, since we can build and rebuild experimental memory systems to evolve something that works.

2. Clocks

A clock, to a Robot, is a sensor that provides time data as HalStreams like any other sensor. Those functions that need time can obtain it, those that don't need time can ignore it. A clock, calendar would be nice. Then we would have: years, months, days, hours, minutes and seconds HalStreams or combinations of these as HalStreams. You only need this if your robot must know what time it is.

Time, of course, is inherent in the Robot, since each HalNode has a processing time c. Hal stream time is future becoming present becoming past every time tick c. The robot is in now, was in past, will be in future.

2. Hearing

We need to relate hearing to speech. That way, the objects hearing seeks are the same as speech produces.

Sound comes in from a digitized microphone. It is pressure amplitude versus time. Amplitude is not very informative and is too variable; too many values mean the same thing. Since we are working with HalStreams, we have no way to do Fourier transforms, since we have no period. We need continuous transforms.

The frequency of the amplitude signal is given by the count of the changes of direction of the derivative of the amplitude curve. Amplitude is sound pressure over time. That is, a sound pressure can be associated with a time. At time t the pressure was x. Frequency is cycles divided by time.

Ears have two functions. One is to provide the direction of sound. For that we need loudness. The other is to decode signals or language. The input to the ear is a single Hal stream.

Frequency is the count of the number of sign changes of d(S) for some time period. The Robot does not need actual frequency. What it needs is an identifier such that the same sound gives the same number. Ears produce a single Hal stream on each side. With a single Hal stream, comparison is differentiation instead of subtraction and addition is integration. We can convert any single Hal stream into as many parallel HalStreams as we wish. It is a process of connecting a string of DNodes and taking the O Hal stream of each as a parallel combinatorial data tree. The simplest serial to parallel is Sound = S - d(S). S is the amplitude Hal stream. d(S) is its rate of change at that point. Subtracting the rate of change from S provides a measure of change.

Here is a truth table of this:

S is a saw tooth wave.

S	d(s)	Sound
0	0	0
1	1	0
2	1	1
3	1	2
2	-1	3
1	-1	2
0	-1	1

S is off-on

S	d(S)	Sound
0	0	0
1	1	0
0	-1	1
1	1	0
0	-1	1
1	1	0
0	-1	1

I think we will find out that Sound is S delayed one cycle, which is a general rule for moving any function backward in time.

Sound[j] = S[j-1] because d(S) = S[j] - S[j-1].

S[j] - d(S) = S[j] - S[j] + S[j-1] = S[j-1].

S is random.

j	S	d(s)	Sound
0	8	0	0
1	3	-5	8
2	9	6	3
3	2	-7	9
4	8	6	2
5	9	1	8

S is 314159

S	d(S)	Sound
3	0	0
1	-2	3
4	3	1
1	-3	4
5	4	1
9	4	5

Works every time.

To expand that, continue adding to this.

d1 = S - d(S) ; S - rate of change of S

d2 = d1 - d2(S) ; d1 - rate of change of d1

Sound = d1 - d2 ; comparison of two rates of change.

This measures two spots on the S Hal stream and Sound is the rate of change of that area.

Here is a truth table for two spots:

d(S) = S[j+1] - S[j]

d2(S) = d(S)[j+1] - d(S)[j]

Sound = d(S)[j] - d2(S)[j]

j	Saw tooth S	d(S)	d2(S)	Sound	off-On S	d(S)	d2(S)	Sound
1	0	0	0	0	0	0	0	0
2	1	1	1	0	1	1	1	0
3	2	1	0	1	0	-1	-2	1
4	1	-1	-2	1	1	1	2	-1
5	0	-1	0	-1	0	-1	-2	1

j	Random S	d(S)	d2(S)	Sound	314159 S	d(S)	d2(S)	Sound
1	8	0	0	0	3	0	0	0
2	2	-6	0	-6	1	-2	-2	0
3	4	2	8	-6	4	3	5	-2
4	0	-4	-6	2	1	-3	-6	3
5	8	8	12	18	5	4	7	-3

To go to three spots, just extend the sequence and the tree.

```
d1 = S - d(S)
d2 = d1 - d(d1)
d3 = d2 - d(d2)
m1 = d1 - d2
m2 = d2 - d3
Sound = m2 - m1
```

By eliminating the m's we find a combinatorial tree.

```
Sound = S - 3*d1 +3*d2 - d3
```

Here are some truth tables of a four input tree from S.

```
S is a sawtooth wave
ds[j+1] = S[j+1] - S[j]
d2s[j+1] = ds[j+1] - ds[j]
d3s[j+1] = d2s[j+1] - d2s[j]
d1[j] = S[j] - ds[j]
d2[j] = ds[j] - d2s[j]
d3[j] = d2s[j] - d3s[j]
m1[j] = d1[j] - d2[j]
m2[j] = d2[j] - d3[j]
Sound = m1 - m2
```

j	S	ds	d2s	d3s	d1	d2	d3	m1	m2	Sound
1	1	0	0	0	1	0	0	1	0	1
2	2	1	1	1	1	0	0	1	0	1
3	3	1	0	−1	2	1	1	1	0	1
4	4	1	0	0	3	1	0	2	1	1
5	5	1	0	0	4	1	0	3	1	2
6	6	1	0	0	5	1	0	4	1	3
7	5	−1	−2	0	6	−3	−2	9	−1	10
8	4	−1	0	2	5	−1	−2	6	1	5
9	3	−1	0	0	4	−1	0	5	−1	6
10	2	−1	0	0	3	−1	0	4	−1	5
11	1	−1	0	0	2	−1	0	3	−1	4

2. Loudness

Loudness can be captured for any number of points. For two points connect an ONode to either side of two PNodes that are passing the S Hal stream.
S is the original sound wave.

s1 = S + k ; k is a volume control. s1 lags behind S
s2 = s1 + k ; s2 lags behind s1
Loudness = s1 o s2
dLoud = s1 - s2

k can be run from outside, setting the volume of S from -128 to 127. Normal is zero. Plus increases. Unlike humans, a Robot can listen more with one ear than the other.

This can be extended for as many sound points as you need. Then you will have a tree of Loudness and a tree of dLoud. Probably this should extend over the duration of the longest phoneme. That should uniquely identify each phoneme. Since we have made a HalTree from a Hal stream we can use all the object detection tools on this HalTree.

S	k	s1	s2	Loud	dLoud	Comments
0	0	0	0	0	0	null
1	0	0	0	0	0	null
2	0	1	0	1	1	Approaching
3	0	2	1	2	1	Approaching
4	0	3	2	3	1	Approaching
3	0	4	3	4	1	Approaching
2	0	3	4	4	-1	Going away
1	0	2	3	3	-1	Going away
0	0	1	2	2	-1	Going away

2. Frequency

The FNode was developed to provide a measure of frequency directly. Freq = f(S) where S is the sound amplitude wave. FNode scales the frequency by 200 to keep it within an 8 bit integer. I can measure frequencies up to 40,000 cycles per second.

Frequency is measured by measuring the time period. We count while d(S) goes plus and minus. Let C = the count and F = the relative frequency. Then F = Fmax/C. F is Fmax when C is one. This sets the scale. FNode Fmax is 255. F is a single Hal stream. For hearing, run it through some PNodes as we did for loudness. Use ONodes and/or ANodes to collect maximum and minimum frequencies over the period of the number of PNodes.

The next step for humanoid Robots is to identify phonemes and create a phoneme Hal stream which, in turn, is concatenated into words and streams of words.

An English version of the International Phonetic Alphabet is reproduced below. The number is added for counting and for possible coding and identification.

No.	IPA CODE	Example	Phonetic Description
1	EY	gAte	
2	EH	gEt	
3	AE	fAt	Front Vowel
4	AA	fAther	
5	AO	lAWn	
6	OW	lOne	
7	UH	fUll	
8	UW	fOOl	
9	ER	mURdER	
10	AX	About	
11	AH	bUt	
12	AY	hIde	
13	AW	hOW	
14	OY	tOY	
15	P	Pack	Unvoiced
16	b	Back	Voiced
17	t	Time	Unvoiced
18	d	Dime	Voiced
19	k	Coat	Unvoiced
20	g	Goat	Voiced
21	f	Fault	Unvoiced Fricative
22	v	Vault	Voiced Fricative
23	TH	eTHer	Unvoiced Fricative
24	DH	eiTHer	Voiced Fricative t
25	s	Sue	Unvoiced Fricative
26	z	Zoo	Voiced Fricative
27	SH	leaSH	Unvoiced Fricative
28	ZH	leiSure	Voiced Fricative
29	HH	How	Whisper Consonant
30	m	suM	Nasal Consonant
31	n	suN	Nasal Consonant
32	NG	suNG	Nasal Consonant
33	l	Laugh	Liquid Semivowels
34	w	Wear	Liquid Semivowels
35	y	Young	Glide Semivowel
36	r	Rate	Glide Semivowel
37	CH	CHar	Affricate Consonant
38	j	Jar	Affricate Consonant
39	WH	WHere	

Ear1.ani
Author: Harold L. Reed
In: {S, k}
Out: {Loudness, dLoud, Freq or Frequency}
s1 = S + k ; k is volume control, + increases, - decreases
s2 = s1 + k
Loudness = s1 o s2 ; s1 is delayed one tick from S
Freq = f(S) ; binary frequency
F1 = Freq + q ;Ser to parallel
F2 = F1 + q
HiFreq = F1 o F2 ; is real frequency, cycles/sec
LoFreq = F1 a F2
; 4 P Nodes, 1 C Node, 1 O Node, 1 A Node,
; 1 F Node, 4 headers
End Ear1

1. Vision

The primary function of vision is to detect objects within a field of view. That is, to separate figure and ground. As always, there are degrees of vision, starting with none and finishing by seeing objects in the moving field of view and integrating them into concepts. Let us be at the viewpoint of the Robot. Get inside it.

With no vision, you are entombed inside a black box. With no sensors, there are no Hal-Streams and you know nothing. Then, after a time, a small hole, a pinhole, is punched in the box, and suddenly you see light. You know day and night. You can randomly hunt light or shade and know to stop when you find it. This is so good that you punch another pinhole and fix both holes up with light sensors, analogue to digital converters and CNodes and motors and stuff and just like that our random seek can become purposeful. Now you know light, dark, and the direction of light and dark. If need be you can seek light or seek dark. An object of uniform reflectance large enough to cover both eyespots will zero out the CNode. Of course, with two eyespots, the object that covers them is the entire field of view. You cannot separate figure and ground because you cannot see outside the figure.

Now you could just start punching more holes at random and hope something falls out. I am sure nature did that for some time. However, nature does something else that works even better. That is to use the same structure but at a different scale. I can look at a few billion years of evolution and copy like mad. As I did for Robots, I will start with the simplest eye and build incrementally so you can see what is happening with each step and how they accumulate.

Eye1 is a single light sensor, L. It provides 256 values of light intensity from 0, no light to 255, maximum light intensity. If we use three sensors, for color then we have intensity for each color, Red, Green and Blue. If we let color be a property of light, then L = Red + Green + Blue, and we are back to light intensity with the property of color. So we still have a one pixel sensor. From now on I will talk about light, understanding that we can color it later.

Eye2 is two light sensors. L and H. Light intensity is preserved. Both L and H provide intensity. Now direction is added to our knowledge. If L is larger than H then there is more light in that direction. We can say: Dir = L - H and

Intensity = L o H.

Eye3 with three light sensors adds very little. Direction and intensity are preserved but the third sensor usually cancels.

Eye4 with four light sensors is the first that can have both figure and ground. The sensors are L2, L1, R1, R2 in that order. Intensity is preserved. Direction is preserved. Figure and ground are now possible, meaning we can detect an object. With an object we can add the color property.

	0	1	2	3
0	R2			
1	R1	n11		
2	L1	n21	n22	
3	L2	n31	n32	n33

The tree algebra with is nodes is:

```
n11 = R1 is R2       ;location  1,  length  1, ground 2
N21 = L1 is R1       ;Location  2,  length  1, ground 2
n31 = L2 is L1       ;location  3,  length  1, ground 2

n22 = n21 is n11     ;location  1,  length  2, ground 1
n32 = n31 is n21     ;location  2,  length  2, ground 1

n33 = n32 is n22     ;location  1,  length  3, ground 0
```

If n33 is 0, there is no object and ground is 3.

You need to pass on the codes for location and length.

Use g nodes for that like:

```
L11 = n11 g 11 ;if nxx > 0, Lxx = xx else Lxx = 0
L21 = n21 g 21
L31 = n31 g 31
```

```
L22 = n22 g 22
L32 = n32 g 32

L33 = n33 g 33
```

Now select max code for each length.

```
Loc1 = L11 o L21 o L31
Loc2 = L22 0 L32
Loc3 = L33
```

Decode length and location.

```
Mcode = Loc1 o Loc2 o Loc3      ;get max code
Length = Mcode and 00001111     ;separate length
and location
Location = Mcode and 11110000 ;codes
```

This is how object length and location are computed. This will be done over later. There are some general things to be discussed.

You need at least two eyes. In each two eyes are two smaller eyes and so on down to the last side by side eye cells. I do this first in one dimension. The cells are side by side like this:

```
L1 R1
|-s-|      s is the distance be-
```

tween sensors.

When you add cells or sensors, they can go like this:

```
L2 L1 R1 R2
```

All sensors are s units apart.

You move. Objects move. When you move, the field moves past us. When an object moves, it moves counter to the field or faster than the field. This is the fact that makes object recognition possible. You are able to pick an object from a field because it moves in the field. Objects of pattern are in the field and are detected because of the sameness of the light density. A rock in a field is a patch of differing light density from the rest of the field. In a typical scene, there are thousands of pattern objects, all moving along with us.

To see this, look out a window and move yourself to the left. Note that everything outside the window also moves to the left relative to the window. The scene moves at the same speed you move. A moving object in the scene moves at a different speed.

Pure rotation in front of the window causes the scene outside the window to move counter to the rotation. Rotate left, the field moves right. Rotate right and the field moves left. Inserting a lens will reverse both directions, so you have to pay attention to the direction, but not too much attention.

Pattern objects move together. Live objects move across the field of pattern objects. Pattern objects are ground to live or moving objects.

Color

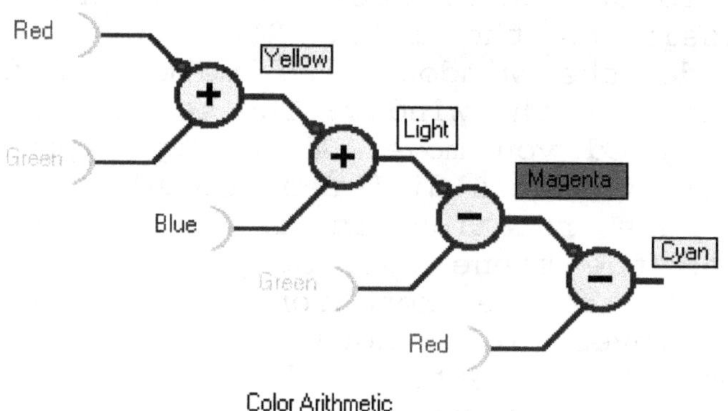

Color Arithmetic

Yellow = Red + Green
Light = Yellow + Blue
Magenta = Light - Green
Cyan = Magenta - Red

Figure 11 Colors

For color vision, all of the innermost sensors are made in triples for Red, Green and Blue. Putting a red filter in front of a sensor makes Red. Using a green and blue filter respectively in front of their sensors makes Green and Blue.

Now all calculations are done for all colors and, in addition, you can have color calculations. There is, of course, a numeric relationship among the colors. I will write the color calculations in general, but remember, they apply to any sensor or sensor combi-

nation. With red, green and blue filters the HalStreams from the sensors are:
Red, Green and Blue.

Red + Green + Blue = Light ; total light
If Red = Green = Blue then Light is White.

Yellow = Red + Green = White - Blue
Magenta = Red + Blue = White - Green
Cyan = Green + Blue = White - Red

Yellow + Magenta + Cyan = Black if Yellow = Magenta = Cyan
These are all the color equations and relationships.

For Robots, you can define color as a property of an object.
White = ISTree(Red, Green, Blue, Light) ; or:

m1 = Red is Green
White = m1 is Blue ; White = Red is Green is Blue

Black = ISTree(Yellow, Magenta, Cyan) ; or:

M1 = Yellow is Magenta
Black = m1 is Cyan ; Black = Yellow is Magenta is Cyan

Light = PTree(Red, Green, Blue)

M1 = Red + Green
Light = M1 + Blue ; Light = Red + Green + Blue

Objects

An object is a self-similar patch of stuff in a field.
Objects have properties that you may or may not need.
Object properties are:

```
Length    ; requires at least one row of horizontal sensors
Height    ; requires at least one row of vertical sensors
Color     ; requires color sensors
Speed     ; a derived property
Direction ; given by eye separation
Intensity ; direct from sensors
Distance  ; a derived property
```

Other properties can be derived from these.

Eye sensors grow in rings. The central ring is:

```
  U1        o
L1  R1 or  o o
  D1        o                 U2
                           d  U1 d
Adding a ring creates  L2 L1 R1 R2
                           d  D1 d
                              D2
```

This leaves space for diagonal sensors to complete the circle. For this exercise, I will leave out the diagonal and the vertical since everything I develop for the horizontal can be replicated for the vertical and diagonals.

So the horizontal slice though our eye after I add L3 and R3 gives us:

```
L3 L2 L1 R1 R2 R3
      |-s-|
```

The sensors L1 to Ln and R1 to Rn are identical and produce a positive integer related to the light intensity. Dark is zero and maximum light is 255. (As an integer, dark is -128 and maximum light is 127.)

The distance between sensors L1 and R1 is s. The distance between R1 and R2 is also s. s is the base of this eye, and is the smallest object that can be detected.

For color, L1, L2, L3 and R1, R2, and R3 are the sum of Red, Green and Blue sensors. They are arranged the same way the sensors were arranged above, but since they take more space, the distance s will be larger. Now, instead of R1 there will be RedR1, GreenR1 and BlueR1.

How they are arranged will matter to color boundaries. Ideally they should be right behind each other, but that is not practical, so we just squeeze them as close as possible. Since we have three sensors, they must be arranged in a triangle, or a line, in some orientation.

In line: R G B I suggest putting green in the middle.

```
R B G    R G B
G R B    B G R
G B R
B G R
B R G
```

In a line, two colors can be cut off by an edge. A white rectangle sweeping by will evoke colors on the edge. So object size is based on the largest distance between sensors.

```
RL GL BL RR GR BR
|_______ s _____|
```

```
In triangle    R   R   G   G   B   B
             G B B G R B B R G R R G
R1G1B1,R1G1B1,...
G2B2R2,G2B2R2,...
 |__ s _|
```

Diode and photo transistors are generally round and can be packed like cans. Filters can be cut to size and placed right on the sensors. We cannot see small objects until the sensor people can make us proper sensors, with access to every pixel.

Color sensors are summed into the L and R total sensors.

YL1 = RedL1 + GreenL1 and L1 = YL1 + BlueL1
YL2 = RedL2 + GreenL2 and L2 = YL2 + BlueL2
YL3 = RedL3 + GreenL3 and L3 = YL3 + BlueL3
YR1 = RedR1 + GreenR1 and R1 = YR1 + BlueR1
YR2 = RedR2 + GreenR2 and R2 = YR2 + BlueR2
YR3 = RedR3 + GreenR3 and R3 = YR3 + BlueR3

If I develop color as an attribute, I only have to triple the sensors. The rest of the computation is done on whole light. Then we don't have to do the computation three times.

You need to seek objects. When an object is found, you need to determine its length and location.

Sensors go up by twos: 2, 4, 6, 8, 10… Number of sensors
Color sensors, up by 6: 6, 12,18,24,30...
Size bits go up by one: 0, 1, 2, 3, 4… Number of pairs
Possible locations go up with sensors.

Draw the tree and attach numbers so we can add length and location codes.

```
S0
S1    n11
S2    n21    n22
S3    n31    n32    n33
S4    n41    n42    n43    n44

n11 = S1 - S0          ;length 1 location 1
n21 = S2 - S1          ;length 1 location 2
n31 = S3 - S2          ;length 1 location 3
n41 = S4 - S3          ;length 1 location 4

n22 = n21 - n11   ;length 2 location 2
n32 = n31 - n21   ;length 2 location 3
n42 = n41 - n31   ;length 2 location 4

n33 = n32 - n22   ;length 3 location 3
n43 = n42 - n32   ;length 3 location 4

n44 = n43 - n33   ;length 4 location 4
```

Now start detection of object size and location.

```
L11 = n11 z 11 ;First level possible objects
L21 = n21 z 21 ;Code is location, length
L37 = n31 z 31 ;Code concatenates, so 1,8 is 18
L46 = n41 z 41

L22 = n22 z 22
L32 = n32 z 32
L42 = n42 z 42

L33 = n33 z 33
L43 = n43 z 43

L44 = n44 z 44

Loc1 = L11 o L21 o L31 o L41
Loc2 = L22 o L32 o L42
Loc3 = L33 o L43
Loc4 = L44

MCode = Loc1 o Loc2 o Loc3 o Loc4
Length = MCode and 0001111  ;240
```

Code is 0 1 2 3 4;

HLoc = MCode and 1111000
Code is 10 20 30 40

Now you have horizontal length and location. If Horizontal length = 0 then there is no object here.
Now duplicate this on the vertical. Call the code UXX instead of LXX. On the vertical we calculate MVCode.

Height = MVCode and 0000111
Code is 1 2 3 4

VLoc = MVCode and 11110000
Code is 10 20 30 40

Now we have a horizontal and vertical slice of the image area plane at this moment.

```
Now: Shape = Length - Height  ; - 0 +
                        ;Tall Square Short
```

You can add **Size = Length * Height** as another property.

```
Location = HLoc - VLoc   ;-   0       +
                        ;up  front    down
```

The color property can be developed along with object detection. If an object has been found then it is of the same color by necessity. For now you can say:

```
Red = RedL1 o RedR1 ; Get color from the inner sensors
Green = GreenL1 o GreenR1
Blue = BlueL1 o BlueR1
M1 = Green + Red
Light = M1 + Blue
Black = Not(Light)

wm1 = Red is Green
White = wm1 is Blue

Rm1 = Red gt Green
Redish = Rm1 gt Blue     ;Red if Red > Green > Blue else 0
Gm1 = Green gt Red
Greenish = Gm1 gt Blue; Green if Green > Red > Blue
Bm1 = Blue gt Red
Blueish = Bm1 gt Green

ColorRG = Redish + Greenish
Color = ColorRG + Blueish

Speed = d(Location)

ThisObject = Size + Shape
Object1 = ThisObject + Location
ColoredObject = Object1 + Color
Object3 = ColoredObject + Speed
Object4 = Object3 + Distance ; If you have distance
Object = Object4 + Sound ; If you have sound
```

Object is the single Hal stream from this network of nodes. At the same time we have the attributes. Next step for these would be to short term memory. Make was and wgt trees beside the is and gt trees.

The objects of this horizontal and vertical eye structure are all colored rectangles, nothing but rectangles. With two eyes they are colored boxes. The smallest rectangle is defined by the smallest distance between color sensors. The eye can be extended in two directions. Add more rings and you have more discrimination. Fill in the diagonal sensors and you have colored polygon objects. Output will be more than length and height. Shape will be a polygon whose shape depends on how we fill the diagonals. Ultimately we should find round objects by filling in the polygon. I took care of motion by making the object detection independent of motion. It does not matter who moves. Movement is relative.

This is the first level of vision. It does not yet provide sight.

1. Rules to Actions

Complex actions can arise from simple beginnings. Following a gradient is one of those simple things that can grow into complex actions. Here is how.

Start with following a gradient, meaning detecting something and going in the direction of greater concentration. Picture a microbe in a dish. Put a drop of sugar in the dish and the microbe will find it as it spreads. The microbe detects a stream of sugar molecules and moves toward the greatest concentration of sugar molecules. Some brain is required for this. Picture a salmon out in the ocean being able to smell its own river among all the other smells. (We will get to that.)

The minimum requirement for following a gradient is two sensors (to detect the gradient) and two motors (to move toward the gradient.)

Two motors mean two functions. We could have a left motor and a right motor which would combine direction and forward motion or we can make a direction function and a motion function or rudder and propeller, to borrow boat terminology.

So we have: rudder = {something} and propeller = {x}.
{Something}, of course, is the two required sensors. We could have SLeft and SRight sensors to detect the content of the gradient.
Let Rudder = Sleft - SRight ; the required brain.
Let propeller = Sleft o SRight ; run if something there.
Now we can follow any gradient that the sensors can detect.

Here is a truth table:

SLeft	SRight	Rudder	propeller
0	0	0	0
0	1	R	1
1	0	L	1
1	1	0	1

Not everything is good to eat. We need to put the other side of following gradients with fleeing gradients. The brain required for this is, naturally, the negative of the following brain.

So there are now two things in this universe. There is the good that we want to seek and the bad that we want to flee.

Again, two sensors are required to detect the bad. Call them BLeft and BRight. Direction of bad is BRight - BLeft. Since we are fleeing, the sensors are transposed from the good sensors. That is the negation.

Now the two sets of sensors must be combined for the rudder and propeller.

Let DGood = Sleft - SRight
Let DBad = BRight - BLeft
Then rudder = DGood o DBad ;
propeller = DGood - DBad ;follow or flee

Here is the truth table for DGood and DBad:

DGood	DBad	Rudder	propeller
0	0	0	0
0	1	1	-1
1	0	1	1
1	1	0	0

Continue this process with sensors between good and bad and you add discrimination and end up with navigating between good and bad again. This is continued and refined in the following.

1. A Robot Microbe

Every living thing is a system containing a set of systems. Every living thing has sensors and motors, producing and eating Hal-Streams. The major systems are control, manufacturing and reproduction.

2. Microbe

To show a control system I apply Hal algebra to the simplest animal, the always-hungry microbe. Every microbe can follow a gradient to find food. How does it do that? Sensors and motors are required and I must do comparison or differentiation. I can apply this to a model microbe. First, the system:

Data Flow: Nature -> Sensors -> Motors -> Nature

I collect objects and actions for the microbe. MS = {Go, food sense1, food sense2} ;defines microbe.

Go = {MR, ML} ; MR and ML are motors.

Food sense1, Food sense2 = {S1,S2} ; are sensors.

SL and SR are positioned on the left and right front of the microbe model. ML and MR are propellers positioned on the left and right rear of the microbe model.

No brain is required for this. Sensors can connect directly to motors.

I start with the motors, always. Here I have two motors to coordinate, but I can still handle them one at a time.

ML = {everything that makes it go forward}
- {Everything that makes it go backward}

MR = {everything that makes it go backward}
- {Everything that makes it go forward}

Design consists of defining the sets {Everything to make it go forward} and {Everything to make it go backward}

The very simplest implementation is to let SR = {Everything to make it go forward} and let SL = {Everything to make it go backward}

Then **ML = SR**
and **MR = SL**
I can look at this as logic.
If SL > SR Then MR > ML and it turns left.
If SR > SL Then ML > MR and it turns right.
If SR = SL Then ML = MR and it goes straight.

All this logic is built into the connections I have made. It rides on free. The dynamic of this is that a new computation is made several thousand times each second. The real microbe continually computes also.

Just as brains slide into sensors and motors, as I go smaller yet, down to the proteins in our microbe I find the sensors, brains and motors are combined into one. Now instead of tracking food, I track electric charge. Discrimination is at a minimum but the action remains.

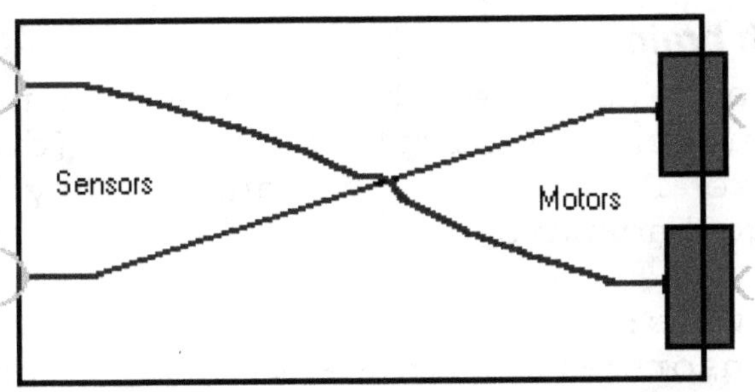

Microbe with null brain

Figure 12 Microbe

2. Microbe with brain

I can add HalNodes to make a brain for this model microbe. I simply expand on {everything to make it go forward} and {everything to make to go backward}

Data Flow now is:
Nature -> Sensors -> Brain -> Motors -> Nature

(I simply insert Brain between Sensors and Motors.)

ML = SR - SL ; Add a CNode
MR = SL - SR ; To each
Again I can examine the free logic.
If SR > SL then ML > 0 and MR < 0 and it turns left
If SL > SR then ML < 0 and MR > 0 and it turns right
If SL = SR then ML = 0 and MR = 0 and it stays put

Note that it no longer has explicit forward or backward motion.

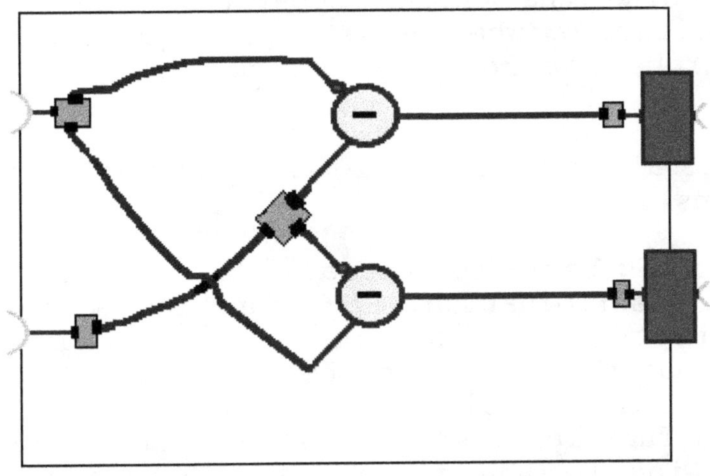

Figure 13 Microbe with brain

I unplug the cables from ML and MR and connect two CNodes between the sensors and motors. Adding the CNodes separates direction from motion. Now when ML is plus, MR is minus. The microbe now rotates, but has no forward motion.

Two general notions arise from adding brain functions.

1. Functions begin to separate. That is, there is more discrimination. Each function becomes a bit in the word that makes up the Robot. Discrimination grows from the number of bits.
2. More brain function is required to restore combined function lost. I need to restore forward motion to the microbe and I have many choices of how to do that, all of them leading into questions of goals. What does the model microbe want to do? Even a microbe has a goal in life. It needs to find food and avoid non-food. When I restore the forward/backward motion, I must consider this.

Forward motion = {all good things} - {all bad things}
or
Seek = Good - Bad ; to be explicit

The microbe brain can be expanded laterally or vertically or both. To expand laterally, add two sensors to detect poison stuff.
SpR and SpL detect bad stuff.
Remember SR and SL detect food or good stuff.
BS = SpR - SpL ; Direction away from poison
GS = SL - SR ; Direction of food
Dir = GS + BS ; general rotation

Here is a truth table for direction:

SpR	SpL	SL	SR	BS	GS	Dir	Comments
0	0	0	0	0	0	0	nothing
0	0	0	1	0	−1	−1	left
0	0	1	0	0	1	1	Right
0	0	1	1	0	0	0	Straight
0	1	0	0	−1	0	−1	Left
0	1	0	1	−1	−1	−2	Left more
0	1	1	0	−1	1	0	Straight
0	1	1	1	−1	0	−1	Left
1	0	0	0	1	0	1	Right
1	0	0	1	1	−1	0	Straight
1	0	1	0	1	1	2	Right more
1	0	1	1	1	0	1	Right
1	1	0	0	0	0	0	Straight
1	1	0	1	0	−1	−1	Left
1	1	1	0	0	1	1	Right
1	1	1	1	0	0	0	Straight

Now to add motion:

```
SG = SL o SR    ; Good is max of food
SB = SpL o SpR  ; Bad is max of poison

Seek = SG - SB  ; Motion
```

Now to combine the two functions:

```
ML = Seek + Dir
MR = Seek - Dir
```

Let's make a truth table to see how this works.

Seek	Dir	ML	MR	Action
-1	-1	-2	0	Rotate CW
-1	0	-1	-1	Go backward
-1	1	0	-2	Rotate CCW
0	-1	-1	1	Rotate CW
0	0	0	0	Do nothing, be happy
0	1	1	-1	Rotate CCW
1	-1	0	2	Rotate CW
1	0	1	1	Go forward
1	1	2	0	Rotate CCW

In a truth table like this, when sensor values are counted up, if we have all the actions the Robot requires, then we are sure they will appear when real data is provided. If they do not appear, then you need to redesign.

Motors are functions and functions are motors. If I have two motors I have two functions, no matter how intermingled they are. No matter how complex the trees that feed a motor, the motor action is that simple to analyze.

The microbe now has speed, direction and discrimination. The closer the sensor values, the slower the speed. Just like before. Now the microbe is responding to the amplitude of the sensors. It sees where, and how much.

To sum:
Sensors are:
SR, SL ; food sensors, right and left
SpR, SpL ; poison sensors, right and left

Motors are:
MR, ML ; Propellers, right and left

The microbe does not need it but I can add pain, hunger and fear as easily as I add any function. This may give us some insight into the mechanism of consciousness. I will have to define what they are to put them in the microbe. This will also scale upwards, so I am not wasting time here.

Pain monitors sensors and motors. If they get out of a specified range, they will modify behavior. For this microbe, I will just run it to a scream motor. The action is:
pain = sensor(s) > pain_set ; pain_set is one of the constants of this microbe system.

Hunger is a measure of the food supply. To provide hunger, I must make the microbe eat. If it eats, it must excrete. This also supplies the energy, the go of the microbe. I will need new motors and sensors.

2. Microbe with goals

I make a new microbe, using some parts of the old where possible.

SG = SL o SR ; Good is max of food
SB = SpL o SpR ; Bad is max of poison

ML = forward - backward
MR = forward - ML
forward = hunger - fear
hunger = waste GT food ; hunger caused by lack of food
food = food plus Eating ; food accumulates by eating
Eating = SG GT SB ; eat only when good
fear = SG - SB

backward = fear GT M11
M11 = hunger o M12
M12 = SB GT M13
M13 = SG o M14
M14 = Pain GT PainThreshold
Pain = SB o waste ; Too much energy or too much poison
waste = ML + MR ; motors use energy.

PainThreshold is a constant now. Every constant can be promoted to a variable at any time by adding HalNodes, and any variable can be demoted to a constant by removing HalNodes.

Looks messy, but that is all right. Like nature I can make circular definitions, have redundant structures and variables and general sloppiness. The advantage of an algebra notation is that I can express structures that are too complex to picture. This cannot be done in a spreadsheet since we are feeding output back to input. It will drive a computer crazy, but with Hal algebra, if you can connect it, it is legal.

When I start to assemble this algebra, like a computer assembler, I find my mistakes and cables with no place to go. Like nature, our design is an iterative process. I must take the place of nature for both learning and evolution, but I can do that. With a common language, Robots can evolve rapidly as new structures are shared.

In a real microbe, this structure is replicated all over its body in sensor, motor pairs. Discrimination, in a microbe, is very fine.

Under this is the machinery of manufacturing and reproduction. With this we make the body, sensors, brain and motors as needed. There is algebra here also. When conditions are right, when we have an excess of parts, we make another microbe and copy the algebra to it. The variables of the brain are defined from here, so this is a lower level still from our microbe brain.

2. Sickness and death

Cells die. So do Robots. What can fail in the Robot are sensors, HalNodes, cables, and motors. As in life, some failures can be tolerated and some failures cause death.

Sensors create HalStreams. If the sensor fails, the Hal stream no longer reflects the original reality. From its position in the tree, the effect may range from unnoticeable to complete function failure.

In the microbe, since it has few sensors, the loss of any one may be catastrophic. A food sensor open will cause the microbe to always seek in that direction, ultimately running around in a circle. Food sensor closed makes it circle in the other direction. The same applies to poison sensors. Two failures could actually counter each other and the Robot would still seem to work.

Hal stream cable can fail with one or more broken wires. Where the wire is located makes the difference in the consequences of failure.

A failure of power is always fatal to that tree or function.
Failure of bit ID will produce on or off constant.
Failure of bit IC is catastrophic. Nodes will hang up.
Failure of ground wire is insanity. All HalStreams become random.

Random bit failures do not bother the Robot at all. We, the designers, need not worry about parity. The Robot can tolerate sloppy sensors and motors that run most of the time.

The failure of any integrated circuits on the HalNode will cause failure of the Hal stream it is emitting. Generally, the Hal stream will be either some constant or open and random. The closer the HalNode is to a motor, the worse the effect of the loss.

Motors generally fail by not running when told to run. A permanent motor failure is always a function failure and is never good. The microbe or Robot may be able to do without the function. Like cables and numbers, functions have a power structure and the failure consequence depends on its position there. There can be cases when failure is running always. That is when the motor controller fails. The motor may run always in a random direction. The effects are complementary.

2. Supply and demand

We can only keep the books for the manufacturing system. We cannot yet make proteins.

Amino Acids -> A protein is very much like P = A + B but it is not arithmetic. The quantities A and B get used up in the process here. But now that we have a language we can say:

P = A a B using an ANode. Then P = min(A,B)

Suppose it requires two A things and 1 B thing to make 1C thing, then to make C, we take 2 things from A and 1 thing from B and combine them into 1 thing in C.

1C = 2A1B. As in a Robot we could write

1C = 2A a 1B to indicate limitation of 1C.

In nature, this is a continuous process. 2A and 1B are HalStreams of quantity information. The limiting conditions are: we run out of A or B or C is at some limit. Of course something is making A and B also, and C is used to make something else, so this is a dynamic process that is regulated by scarcity and rates of production. There are loops here also. For example, B might be built from C. 1C = 2A and 1C or 1C = 2A a 1C. Water = 2H a 1O. (2H1O is much easier to write than H_2O.) Of course H = 1p1e, H is one proton and one electron and O = 8p8e where p is proton and e is electron.

I do not want to get into chemistry here and I do not have Hal Nodes that do chemical arithmetic, although it is something to think about. Actually A Nodes can do chemical combination calculations.

What I can do is monitor quantities of A, B or C. That is, I make a sensor that can count C and create a Hal stream of C. Now we can do arithmetic. As quantities of C go up, quantities of A and B go down in the fixed relationship I have already established. Now you can write 1C = 2A a 1B to compute the quantity of 1C produced.

2. A Machine Neuron

Since a neuron is a HalTree we need only to make a tree. Let the dendrites have one synapse. I will make a six dendrite neuron that internally is two three input trees connected to a CNode. Let O be the axon of the neuron. Name the synapses on the positive side L1, and L2. Name the synapses on the negative side R1, and R2. So now we have:

O = f(L1,L2) - q(R1,R2)

The function f can be either a collector or selector, an aggregator or chooser. To aggregate let A = L1 + L2 and

B = R1 + R2

Then O = A - B

To choose, let A and B be ONodes.

A = L1 o L2 and B = R1 o R2

Depending on the physical orientation of the synapses, both these methods compute direction of the highest input. What this means is determined by the context the neuron is in, what its input providers are doing.

To measure change, use CNodes and let:

A = L1 - L2 and B = R1 - R2

If the synapses were binary, (they cannot be) we can write a truth table for all these.

L1	L2	R1	R2	A+	Ao	A-	B+	Bo	B-	O+	Oo	O-
0	0	0	0	0	0	0	0	0	0	0	0	0
0	0	0	1	0	0	0	1	1	-1	-1	-1	1
0	0	1	0	0	0	0	1	1	1	-1	-1	-1
0	0	1	1	0	0	0	2	1	0	-2	-1	0
0	1	0	0	1	1	1	0	0	0	1	1	1
0	1	0	1	1	1	1	1	1	-1	0	0	2
0	1	1	0	1	1	-1	1	1	1	0	0	-2
0	1	1	1	1	1	-1	2	1	0	-1	0	-1
1	0	0	0	1	1	1	0	0	0	1	1	0
1	0	0	1	1	1	1	1	1	-1	0	0	2
1	0	1	0	1	1	1	1	1	1	0	0	0
1	0	1	1	1	1	1	2	1	0	-1	0	1
1	1	0	0	2	1	0	0	0	0	2	1	0
1	1	0	1	2	1	0	1	1	-1	1	0	-2
1	1	1	0	2	1	0	1	1	1	1	0	0
1	1	1	1	2	1	0	2	1	0	0	0	0

The arithmetic remains, having meaning only when in a connected structure.

2. Recap and on to Robots

It is about time to go do some applications, so it would be good to review what we have done.

We have learned that numbers are invisible and arise from actions of counting and arithmetic. We have seen that every number symbol can be written as a single digit. Digits cycle, therefore all numbers must cycle. No infinite numbers here.

Making number symbols move created Hal Streams. Hal Streams complete arithmetic and incorporate calculus as a basic part of Hal stream arithmetic with next number replacing next infinitesimal position on the curve.

We have seen that arithmetic addition and subtraction are the same as integration and differentiation, except that arithmetic works in space and calculus works in time. Since time and space can be interchanged, so can arithmetic and calculus. a = b + c, a = i(b)-c. a = b - c, a = d(b). Note that differentiation removes a variable and integration adds a variable.

We have defined functions as variable equations and have explored possible logic functions.

We have introduced sensors, to produce Hal Streams and motors to read Hal Streams. Both are familiar terms to robot builders and engineers. However these are new objects in mathematics, and they are just as abstract as lines and points.

All this together is a tool to create action models of anything. We no longer need to solve problems. The problems we are interested in now mostly have no simple solutions. The Hal algebra equations are to build the machine to compute a solution to the problem. This provides understanding of a different kind. We have learned a Robot programming language and have applied some of it to trees and numbers. The software of the Robot is nature. We write a program in Hal algebra to build the machine that nature programs.

We have discovered that HalTrees are neurons, giving us a biological field to play in.

The time has come to put all this together and go out and apply it to the world. Bravely we step into the world of the Robot.

1. Building Robots

From here on we are devoted to building a series of Robots, starting with the smallest and ending with a human sized Robot. As we need them, I will stop and create assemblies, or agents for eyes and ears.

You have seen Hal algebra and now it is time to put it to work. Designing Robots with Hal algebra is similar to writing a computer program in that you write code. The differences are that Hal algebra code assembles machines where computer code assembles machine code, and Hal algebra nodes all work at the same time, so there is no sequence, while computer code is full of sequence and sequence changing codes.

Hal algebra can be written on a napkin, but to look to the future, I will set some style rules.

If your purpose is to explain a Robot to another person, then just be literary.

If you are assembling a Robot, make the code like a computer program in that you assume a computer will read it. That means it has to be properly delimited so the stupid computer can pick the code out of the text.

Why does a computer need to read the code? Later on there will be a development system so that you can write your code and have a HalNode and cable list pulled out of it. The development system might even try to run the code as a simulation. So, for forward compatibility, write your code properly.

What is proper is to write one HalNode equation on a line with any associated comment separated by a semicolon (;). Then the HalNode count is the line count. This is Robot machine code you are writing, you cannot get any lower.

Use the convention of writing code in the form:
Motor = sensor1 - sensor2 ; where output is on the left of the equal sign and inputs are on the right. You will be counting motors and sensors until the development system does it for you. The development system should provide you with a HalNode list, a variable list, and a cable list with the plugs needed on each cable, a motor list and a sensor list. The HalNode and cable list is a parts list for the brain. The motor list and sensor list are connections to the body.

Now that we are writing code, I will go through the HalNode list with comment relating to coding or programming.

Sensors connect to the body. A sensor should be dumb. It should be numeric with at least three bits in the Hal stream it produces so we can do arithmetic (two bits is the limit). The HalStreams from most real sensors will be offset binary. That means there are no negative numbers in the stream.

Every HalNode is also a sensor. The Hal stream coming from a HalNode is at least eight bit numeric.

NNode is used to change the sign of an integer Hal stream. It is a function: **O = n(I)** ; If I is positive, then O is negative else if I is negative then O is positive.

NotNode is used to reverse the logic of a Hal stream.

O = Not(I) ; if I is zero then O is last I else O is 0

PNode is used when you want to aggregate HalStreams and are not interested in the direction of original data but are interested in quantity. We are now combining two HalStreams into one. The notation is infix: **O = L + R** ; Note that a PNode can make a number larger than its capacity so it will roll over.

INode is an integrator. It is used when you need to count up. It is expressed as a function:

O = i(I) ; It is fully equivalent to O = ∫I ; To provide the integration constant, use any external node in series. To add a constant, K, for example use O = i(I) + K

CNode is the original HalNode and the master of all. It has an infix notation:

O = L - R ; Use a CNode when you need to compare two HalStreams or need to determine direction. Good style is to put a CNode on every real motor that has direction and then fill out the tree to I and the tree to R.

DNode is back to single Hal stream but it follows CNode since they are sisters. It is a function: **O = d(I)** ; It is used when you want to know the rate of change of a Hal stream. It is full equivalent to O = dI/dt but dt is always = 1 in a Hal stream, and the notation is simpler.

ONode is a two input HalNode. It has infix notation like:
O = L o R ; Use it to select the largest data from two HalStreams. It is used when you are interested in anyone who speaks the loudest. A tree of ONodes will find the loudest shouter.

ANode is the opposite of the ONode. Its notation is:
O = L a R ; Use it to pick the smallest data from two HalStreams. A tree of ANodes will find the smallest.

GTNode is something that is not in Boolean algebra. It has two inputs but works on a single Hal stream. I use an infix notation: **O = L > R** ; It is a logic HalNode. You can also use: **O = L gt R** ; Use it when you want a HalNode to have no effect (be zero) unless some threshold is passed. Here is the logic of the GTNode:
If L > R then O = L else O = 0 ; So O is zero until L is greater than R. This is used a lot as a pain detector where R is set at some pain threshold and O is the pain.
Pain = condition > pain threshold.

LTNode is the less than version logic nodes. Its notation is: **O = L < R** ; or use: **O = L lt R** .

ISNode is the equal version of logic nodes. Its notation is: **O = L is R** ; Is being used for equals. The logic is: If L equal R then O = L else O = 0. Use an ISNode if you are identifying whether two objects are the same. Use a chain of ISNodes to determine if n objects are the same. A tree of ISNodes will determine when every input is the same.

WasEQ is the past tense of ISNode. O = L waseq R is a notation. It returns L if I=R else return last L.

WasGT, and WasLT are the L > R and L < R units.

ZNode is a detection HalNode. It has two inputs and an infix notation but it is not a tree HalNode, but a switch. Notation is: **O = L z R** ; It is a zero detector. What it does is to shout a code or turn on a Hal stream when it sees a zero. Logically, if L = zero then O = R else O = zero.

GNodes is the second of three detection HalNodes. It is: **O = L g R** ; When L is > 0, O = R, else O = 0.

LNode is the final detection HalNode. It is:
O = L l R ; When L is < 0, O = R else O = 0.

Note that R can be a constant code or a full Hal stream in any of these detection HalNodes.

There are **DZ, DG, DL** versions of these switches which test the derivative of L for the condition and returns R if the condition is met.

There are **Wasz, Wasg, Wasl** and **Wasdz, Wasdg, and Wasdl** memory node switches here as well.

AndNodes are for decoding detection codes. They are Boolean and for HalStreams. O = L and R. Either L or R can be a mask to remove bits from the other Hal stream. If the code is 91 then O = 91 and 01 extracts 1. O = 91 and 90 extracts 9. Work in binary with this one.

MPY and **DIV** do exactly that if you need them. DIV is an integer divide.

Refer to this or Hal HalNode introduction to assist in coding.

2. Design notes

With Hal algebra, design is simplified in several ways, although, making a Robot is never easy. Design starts with an idea. The Robot you are designing will have some goals and wishes to work at. You the designer should never make the mistake of trying to tell a Robot what to do. This is why robotics never flew. You create the Robot in such a way that nature tells it what to do. That way you avoid the if-then list and the always forgotten exception.

Designing a Robot should start with defining the motors. This defines what it can do, what its actions are. Then each motor is connected to a CNode and design is accomplished by filling in the plus and minus sides of the CNode. This can be done independently for each motor, so design can proceed in parallel groups. Groups communicate in terms of Hal stream variables. Of course you can also start at the sensors and work toward the motor just as well, or do both. You are always making a direction, collection, detection or command HalTree.

Given a motor, fill in all the things that make it go one way and all the things that make it go the other way. At first this can be just lists of variables. Then, gradually the variables become cables as you connect the tree.

At the leaves of the trees are the actual sensors. They should be in mind in your original design desires. Sensors fetch data from nature and encode it. They provide the program the Robot executes.

All this is easier and more casual than writing a computer program. It makes absolutely no difference in what order you write the code. You can assume that data is always going to be available everywhere, always.

You cannot do this in a word processor, but also draw the nodes and cables and you have a flow diagram that is exact and absolute. (Maybe the development system will let you do that in the computer.) Also, you will quickly find out that Hal algebra can make more complex structures than you can draw easily. (Mainly because algebra is 3d and drawing is 2d.)

Some tips on naming Hal stream variables have come from experience. With variable names you will need to identify body parts, the actions of body parts, and the location (left, right, up, down, fore and aft) of body parts and it helps to do them in that order. Suppose you have some legs and leg joints. Leg joints are hinges that bend. You have left and right legs, at least. Since it is the leg joints that bend, we can leave off designating leg itself, leaving the joints to be established.

Make up a code list, so you do not have to write knee or hip or ankle every time. Make a code list for left, right and so on. Post this to everyone involved.

Then code for knee bending will look like:

knBendingL = knBendL - knNotBendL ; Just use enough to identify this HalNode always.

To recap:

Name variables with Object + action + location and they will segue right into language. Action will be like Do on the input side of the HalNode and like Doing on the output side.

ObjDoingL = ObjDoL - ObjNotDoL ; for example. If there is no question about what is acting, or where, you can leave it off and simply write **Doing = Do - Don't** ; where Do can be any verb you need.

1. Old Engineering -> New Engineering

Engineering is the process of creating systems. Today, most dynamic systems are built with microcontrollers using IF - THEN logic. The embedded computer generally controls Boolean variables that come from sensors and go to motors. Most systems have a human in the control loop somewhere. There will be a shift away from that as we learn to build brains.

The father of all dynamic systems is the clock. The father of control systems is the governor or speed controller, an invention of the steam engine era. It is also the first Robot. As an early control system, it bridges both the control and the Robot worlds, just as Pythagoras bridged East and West and Mathematics and Magic. The automata of the 1700's were mechanical, clockwork Robots.

The thermostat is the first electrical Robot although it is not pure, since it has an operator input.

Appliances are pre Robots. Most have operator controls. Hal stream flow in general is:

Operator -> Sensors -> Motors -> Operator

Conventional Refrigerators, Stoves, Washing machines are all built with "embedded" computers, using register logic.

Sensors -> Registers -> Computer -> Register -> Motors

HalNodes and cables can replace all computer logic and permit engineering to concentrate on sensors and motors. There is no reason a refrigerator cannot be aware of what it is doing. Of course, there is no reason it should either. A machine should be designed to do its job and nothing more.

New appliances will be self-sufficient Robots, and they will need to know what they are doing. Here, the application of Hal stream algebra will be required. I leave old appliances to history. If - then logic works fine to make appliances and computers. I need to go beyond that.

To show off, I will repeat the clock, the governor, and the thermostat with HalNodes.

First the clock:

Clock = amplitude - Clock ; produces square waves of size amplitude. Period is c, the cycle time of the HalNode.

Another clock:

Clock = i(rate) - constant ; produces triangular waves of period 256*c. constant shifts the stream forward or backward.

Now the governor:

SpeedChange = SpeedWanted - SpeedNow

This is a description of every speed controller. It is also a list of HalNodes and cables needed to build them. The engineering now consists of providing the sensors SpeedWanted and SpeedNow and building the motor SpeedChange. The design required is to insure that SpeedChange moves nature to satisfy SpeedNow. Sensors and motors are built into the machine. The control is universal.

And the thermostat:

HeatPumpChange = TemperatureWanted - TemperatureNow ; tells heat pump how to run. Again, the engineering consists of making the heat pump cool if TemperatureNow > TemperatureWanted and heat if TemperatureWanted > TemperatureNow.

Hal algebra is new in the sense it has never been taught in school. It is old in that nature provides the program to operate life and Robots have the same data flow. What the engineer must learn is to see sensors emitting HalStreams and how to arrange the arithmetic so the Robot can react to nature, and to your commands, since you are nature to the Robot.

HalStreams never stop and life does not sit around and calculate where it is. With Hal algebra you have a tool to build Robots, but, like any tool, you must learn to use it. I spent 35 years looking for this, and I am not surprised that engineers cannot see it. Building brains is hard. Building them without a system is impossible.

2. Robot Bodies and Hardware

Building bodies for Robots is almost another subject, but I will make note of a few things here. In algebra a motor can be anything. In a body a motor must be engineered to do the motor action.

Sensors exist half in the body and half in nature. The nature part must be engineered to produce a Hal stream. Sensors should be dumb, just pumping out data. Data width should be two bits or more. Generally eight bits is plenty.

Robot bodies must hold sensors, brain and motors and itself. Bodies should be as light as possible, simply from a power standpoint since moving more mass requires more power.

Moving parts should be simplified to their essence. Robots will have propulsion motors and motors that move the Robots own parts, including other motors. The propulsion can be wheels, propellers or leg bends. The brain does not care what a motor does. It tells something to run. It cannot, and should not know what is running. That means that brains can be transferred from Robot to Robot and still retain their function. That is universality. That is simply mathematics.

There are rotating parts like wheels and propellers. There are positioning things like rudders and other servos. Elbows require a hinge and a motor to open and close the hinge. This could be a servo operation also.

Stay away from the machine shop with Robots. Build them like model airplanes from balsa wood or light plastic. Use hardware store hinges for joints. Use model airplane servos for all your servo jobs. Use gear train motors for rotary parts. If you are rich, you can use linear motors for motion and push-pull. Eventually, you will be able to buy standard parts from various suppliers. There will be standard elbows, feet, knees and so on with built in motors and CNodes. There will be standard eyes, based on discrimination, that produce objects and object properties. A universal language requires a universal hardware set and will cause the hardware to be built. All this is easily done with present technology.

To get all this going, we must all use a common language for design and a standard wiring for HalStreams connectors. That is why Hal algebra is free and node specifications are open and shown. What you must buy is hardware, sensors, motors, HalNodes and Hal Agents.

Now we can go on and build some simple Robots. As we go we will learn how to establish new Hal stream variables and to add brain function at will. What we are programming is not the behavior of the Robot. We provide goals and wishes to the Robot to promote the behavior. Right now we are at the machine language level. Later on we will be able to build compilers that will take goals and wishes and produce the assembly instructions. Very much later on we will have machines that take in code and produce hardware. Insert the code and out pops a Robot. Note that somehow we will always have to produce the code. We are at the very beginning of this, so we will learn as we go. Right now, everything looks like a computer. When everything looks like a Robot, we will have arrived at the next stage of civilization.

I will mention bodies only when required while designing the sample Robots. Keep in mind that they all have bodies and bodies set many parameters.

Remember the data flow:

Nature -> Sensors -> Brain -> Motors -> Nature

2. A1 The Littlest Robot (1,0,1)

This is a Robot only in the sense there must be a least one. We start with the smallest possible structure. One sensor and one motor. Think of it as a microbe that has developed a single light sensitive spot or as a computer going native. The body of this Robot and of those to come is just a rectangular, thin box with rounded corners. Sensors, brain and motors are simply connected on the top of the box. This Robot has a single sensor in the middle and a single propeller in the center rear. If we express code as actions, we can ignore the actual hardware. All actions and object ultimately result in sensors and motors, so we can write a classification scheme that may capture the essential data about the Robot. To do that simply write down the number of sensors, the number of neurons, and the number of motors like this: (S,N,M) where S is number of sensors, N is number of neurons and M is number of motors. Here we have (1,0,1).

```
A1 = (sensor, motor} ; objects
```

sensor = run ; could be light sensor. 0 = dark

Motor = running ; runs propeller

running = run ; is the machine

(Note that the microprocessor equation is of the same form. Decode = Fetch ;is the guts of the computer.)

Make a truth table for offset binary.

Offset binary

run	**running**	
0	0	; stop
1	1	; run
2	2	; run faster
		; crash is the end result

This boat runs toward light always. The closer it gets to the light, the brighter the light becomes. This is feedback through nature. A1 cannot turn and it will accelerate until it crashes once it sees a light. The light must find it, A1 cannot look for light. Neither can the computer. Given data from nature, the computer will always crash.

2. A2 Smallest Brain (1,1,1)

Now add the smallest brain, a BNode. Like all brains, it goes between sensor and motor.

A2 = {sensor, BNode, motor}
sensor = run ; is light sensor ; 0 is dark

motor = running ; runs propeller, forward or backward

running = b(run) ; we make an integer

The truth table
offset

run	**running**	
0	-1	; Go back
1	0	; Stop, be happy
2	1	; go forward

This boat backs away from light until it is dark. We save the light and this machine will stay at a fixed distance from the light based on the sensitivity of its sensor. It has a center. Even this simple structure is beyond the computer.

2. A3 is two dimensional (2,2,2)

Now we can graduate to two sensors, implying two HalStreams or two light spot sensors. This is the first purposive behavior we can see. We retain the boat. The light sensors go on the front corners. Now we can add a rudder for direction change. We also have our first physical parameter. Changing the distance of the eye spots changes the scale of the world A3 sees. A new action is added also.

A3 = {sensors, brain, motors}
sensors = {turnL, turnR} ; are light sensors.
; dark is 0
brain = {CNodes}
motors = {rudder, propeller}
actions = [turning, running

turning = turnL - turnR ; rudder goes left or right and will steer left or right if moving.
running = turnR - turnL ; propeller goes forward or backward For right now I will just make it the negative of rudder.

Make a truth table for that. To be sure the sensors see every combination of input, start with the lowest value and count up. That way you cycle through all possible numbers and you can begin to see that each sensor is a digit in the number, so any time you add a sensor, you add a digit to the number count and you double the possible actions. (This is what kills IF - THEN logic.)

turnL	turnR	turning	running	turn	go
0	0	0	0	no turn	stop
0	1	-1	1	right	forward 1
0	2	-2	2	right	forward 2
1	0	1	-1	left	back 1
1	1	0	0	no turn	stop
1	2	-1	1	right	forward 1
2	0	2	-2	left	back 2
2	1	1	-1	left	back 1
2	2	0	0	no turn	stop

We get a lot more action here just by doubling the sensors. Here each sensor had 3 values but we end up with 9 values of turning. With eight bit sensors, turnL and turnR can each have 256 values and the combination is 65536 actions.

The motor, running, could be done better. Note that the two motors are independent of each other although they share the same sensors. Each motor can be optimized for the best Robot behavior without regard to the other motors. That means each motor could be worked on by an individual team, each bettering their motor within the constraints of the system.

Generally, single motors can be done on spread sheets. Write code, write spreadsheet, test some input and continue this until it seems to work. Then it can go to hardware, first on the bench, then into the Robot. (If the structure is very good and useful, can it into a Hal Agent and sell it.)

The rudder on the boat is all right. The propeller needs to be thought about. It is all right here in that it stops when the sensors are happy. There will be no crashes due to unsatisfied goals. Movement while not turning could be better.

Each motor should be designed to accomplish its own goal. You can use the sensors of other motors if you need them, but generally every motor should have its own sensor tree.

Always let m = {Plist} - {Mlist}, then you can simply add all {Plist} variables and {Mlist} variables together. {Plist} generally will mean forward or right and {MList} will generally mean backward or left in a mobile Robot, although they can have any meaning. Here are two ways of establishing variables from lists.

```
turning = {L} - {R} ; generic
{L} = turnL
{R} = turnR
turning = turnL - turnR   ; specific

running = f - b     ;variables
f = {runforward}    ;{tree list} better. Takes
less code.
b = {runback}
```

With running we are getting in the area of goal satisfaction. What we want propeller to do depends on how we want it to behave.

2. A4 has goals and emotions (2,4,2) -> (8,8,7)

Keeping the same boat from A3, lets add some variables for good and bad. First we will use a constant Hal stream to show how one can set a fixed goal for a Robot.
A4Objects = {rudder, propeller, TurnL ,TurnR, hunger, fear}
A4Actions = {turning, running}

We have already:
turning = TurnL - TurnR
We need to fill:
running = f - b
Let
f = hunger ; initially a constant = h
Let
b = fear ; how about fear of light
m1 = TurnL o TurnR ; take max light. Use an ONode here
fear = m1 > k ; make k a constant = k. Use a GTNode here.

Note, h and k are number pad sensors. They provide a constant Hal stream of any value keyed in. Try letting k = 1 and h = 2.

For the truth table let sL = TurnL and sR = TurnR

The truth table:

sL	sR	m1	k	h	fear	turning	running	
0	0	0	1	2	0	0	2	; forward
0	1	1	1	2	0	-1	2	; forward
0	2	2	1	2	2	-2	0	; stop
1	0	1	1	2	0	1	2	; forward
1	1	1	1	2	0	0	2	; forward
1	2	2	1	2	2	-1	0	; stop
2	0	2	1	2	2	2	0	; stop
2	1	2	1	2	2	1	0	; stop
2	2	2	1	2	2	0	0	; stop
3	3	3	1	2	3	0	-1	; backward

Note that we stick around the constant h. That sets the brightness allowed. In other words the goal for this Robot in regard to light is h. The other side of this goal is k. Change either and the goal set point changes. (In fact, when I first made this truth table both k and h were 1. When I saw it was going backward too soon for me, I changed h to 2 and got it closer to the bright. In practice, h and k are number pad sensors and can easily be set to any of their 256 values. Of course you can add brain to set these dynamically.

This is the first goal seeking behavior. Any Robot exhibits some behavior pattern, whether we code it or not. Hook a bunch of nodes at random and something will happen. You cannot, physically, make an illegal structure. In very complex machines we put in goals and wishes and hope for the best. The light sniffing behavior of this Robot just sort of grew with the improvement of running.

Robot behavior depends on all its sensors and brain nodes. The behavior of each motor is known exactly. The behavior of any sensor is known exactly. The behavior of every HalNode is known exactly but knowing the behavior of a complex robot is more psychology than engineering, simply because of the combinatorial possibilities of many sensors, nodes and motors.

But small Robots we can know exactly and can make truth tables and spreadsheets of them at will. And you should know that big Robots are made of small Robots.

Back to the Robot boat A3. We could improve its vision, since it only has two eye spots, or one eye spot per eye.

Lets give it another eye spot in each eye. Then we have:

A(442) = {eyes, rudder, propeller, hunger, fear}

eyes = {sLL, sLR, sRL, sRR}

These are spaced like:

sLL-sLR-----------------sRL-sRR

Now give each eye a motor, so it can scan.

```
eL = sLL - sLR ; Left eye seeks zero
eR = sRL - sRR ; Right eye seeks zero

turning = eL + eR ; make up rudder
```

Truth table of eyes:

sLL	sLR	sRL	sRR	eL	eR	turning	
0	0	0	0	0	0	0	; all dark
0	0	0	1	0	-1	-1	
0	0	1	0	0	1	1	
0	0	1	1	0	0	0	; right eye
0	1	0	0	-1	0	-1	
0	1	0	1	-1	-1	-2	
0	1	1	0	-1	1	0	
0	1	1	1	-1	0	-1	; right eye
1	0	0	0	1	0	1	
1	0	0	1	1	-1	0	
1	0	1	0	1	1	2	
1	0	1	1	1	0	1	
1	1	0	0	0	0	0	; left eye
1	1	0	1	0	-1	-1	
1	1	1	0	0	1	1	
1	1	1	1	0	0	0	

Now turning needs to be improved. We want to point toward the brightest area and eL and eR do not add up to that. What we need is to find the brightest spot and help the eyes locate zero. We need turning to be a tree of ONodes on both sides.

m1 = sLL o sLR ; max of eL

m2 = sRL o sRR ; max of eR

turning = m1 - m2

the truth table

sLL	sLR	sRL	sRR	m1	m2	turning
0	0	0	0	0	0	0
0	0	0	1	0	1	-1
0	0	1	0	0	1	-1
0	0	1	1	0	1	-1
0	1	0	0	1	0	1
0	1	0	1	1	1	0
0	1	1	0	1	1	0
0	1	1	1	1	1	0
1	0	0	0	1	0	1
1	0	0	1	1	1	0
1	0	1	0	1	1	0
1	0	1	1	1	1	0
1	1	0	0	1	0	1
1	1	0	1	1	1	0
1	1	1	0	1	1	0
1	1	1	1	1	1	0

That looks better. Both eyes and rudder now are seeking light. The difference is that eyes are now seeking a lighted space, not a light spot. We have added a dimension to the Robot's vision. Vision is the separation of figure and ground. We now have ground. This, of course, is how vision evolved. Start with an eye spot. Then two eye spots. Then replicate that so that eye spots grow in pairs and pairs of pairs. 1 2 4 8 16 etc.

Now lets recap this Robot in code form.

A4
eL = sLL - sLR ; wants zero
eR = sRL - sRR ; wants zero
m1 = sLL o sLR ; wants max
m2 = sRL o sRR ; wants max
turning = m1 - m2 ;wants zero of max
running = hunger - fear ; wants zero
hunger = h ; variable substitution, sets hunger
m3 = m1 o m2 ; wants max
fear = m3 > k ; sets fear value if m3 > k

We end up with 10 sensors, 8 motors, 8 nodes and 18 variables. Variables = sensors + motors or sensors + nodes. propeller retains its behavior although we had to change its sensors. Fear is now fed by a tree of ONodes instead of by a single sensor. That itself will make subtle changes in overall behavior but we will still stick around hunger (h) and fear (k).

Lets finish this as if we were going to build A4. There is a set pattern for doing that.

Motors:

eL is a rotary motor. Turns to the value of eL.

eR is a rotary motor. Turns to the value of eR.

turning is a servo motor. Turns to the value of rudder.
running is a rotary motor. It turns at the speed and direction of propeller.
m1, m2 and m3 are virtual motors, collecting values.
7 motors

<u>Sensors:</u>

sLL, sLR, sRL, sRR are light sensors. Dark is zero and bright is 255.
hunger and **fear** are constants.
h and k are number pads
8 sensors

Cables:

variable	plugs	qty
sXX	2	4
mx	3	3
h,k	2	2

nodes	qty
CNode	4
ONode	3
GTNode	1
Power	1

8 nodes

This parts list can be derived from the Robot equations always. The number of plugs on cables is hardest to do, but if you need this you can go to the Robot under construction and measure cable and count plugs. Plugs can be inserted anywhere on a cable and you can use strain relief plugs on the ends. The plug count is related to the number of variables that cable connects. The spacing of the plugs must be done on the Robot. Each variable owns its cable forever. If the scope of the variable changes then the cable must change.

The ultimate project specialization would be to assign a variable to each engineer. Next is to assign one side of a motor, then an entire motor, then an entire Hal Agent and finally, the entire Robot.

Let us make one more addition to the boat Robots to make a point before we go to walking Robots which are mechanically complex to start. What I am doing is adding a motor to A4 which will collect and respond to the status of the machine. I will also add pain, joy and a smile motor.

A4
eL = sLL - sLR ; wants zero
eR = sRL - sRR ; wants zero
m1 = sLL o sLR ; wants max
m2 = sRL o sRR ; wants max
turning = turnL - turnR
turnL = m1 + turnPainL
turnR = m2 + turnPainR
turnPainL = turning > turnlimitp ; pain is turning past
turnPainR = turning < turnlimitn ; limits
turnJoy = turning z turnjoycode ; joy is not having to turn

running = runF - runB ;
runF = joy + hunger ; joy is positive feedback here
runB = fear + Pain
runJoy = runB z runJoyCode ;runjoy is no fear, no pain

hunger = h ; variable substitution, sets hunger
m3 = m1 o m2 ; wants max
fear = m3 > k ; sets fear value if m3 > k

Collect pain
PainLeft = turnPainL ;we might want to collect all left
PainRight = turnPainR ; and all right pains
Pain = PainLeft + PainRight

Note that as we go down the collection tree we become more general. Pain is more general than painLeft which is more general than turnPainL. The property tree is full of information that we can collect in any form for the Robot. This Robot does not need Painleft and PainRight but I provided them to prove a point.

```
Collect joy
Joy = turnJoy + runJoy
```

Collect status

```
status = good - bad ;
 good = Joy + hunger
 bad = Pain + fear  ;

Show emotion
Smile = status ;negative smile is a frown

Set constants
h = 50    ; k = 25
TurnLimitp = 100
turnLimitn = -100
turnJoyCode = 100
runJoyCode = 100
```

This Robot does not have a lot of status to collect. The general idea here is that on any Robot you can collect motor data for status and feedback. What you collect depends on what you have to collect from and what you want it to represent to the Robot. You can make a motor to show that. In this case a servo dial marked in degrees of good and bad would do. In a human type machine the status motors would cause facial changes that could be interpreted as emotion. In fact, emotions are just Hal stream variables that produce an action and are not themselves monitored.

There are several constants in the Robot that we can set with number pads. In a more complex Robot these number pads might be promoted to HalNodes and the setting would depend on a higher level of parameters.

2. A5 gets color vision

Now, instead of eye spots, we can use eyes. Buy two eyevh3 agents and call them eyeL and eyeR. These look like original sensors as far as A5 is concerned. All it has to know is how to associate sensor name with Hal Agent header. For one thing, the Hal Agent, eye, should have names printed next to each header. When we buy the eyes, we should establish Hal Agent output names. Then they can be associated with sensor names in A5.

Establish the two eyes on the boat at each front corner. Remember, the distance apart sets the scale A5 sees. Now we have sensors of LengthL, LenghtR, HeightL, HeightR, HLocationL, HLocationR, VLocationL, VLocationR, IntensityL, IntensityR, ColorL and ColorR from the eye output. These are codes representing lengths, intensity and color.

0 10 20 30 40 50 60 70 80 90 are codes for size.

0 1 2 3 4 5 6 7 8 9 are codes for location.

ShapeL = LengthL - HeightL ; is a code
ShapeR = LengthR - HeightR ; is a code

SizeL = LenghtL + HeightL ; is a code,
;0 1 2 3 4 5 6
SizeR = LengthR + HeightR ; is a code,
;0 1 2 3 4 5 6
ZSize = SizeL - SizeR ; -6 -5 -4 -3 -2 -1
;0 1 2 3 4 5 6
Size = SizeL o SizeR ; 0 1 2 3 4 5 6

HLocation = HLocationL + HLocationR
VLocation = VLocationL + VLocationR

Color = ColorL o ColorR ; Color should be the ;same in each.
Intensity = IntensityL o IntensityR
dIntensity = IntensityL - IntensityR

Now turning can seek any or all of these properties. Or we can make **turning = Shape**. Now instead of seeking light spots we are seeking similar shapes. And propeller now can seek or avoid shapes or size or color.

running = run - notrun
run = rm1 - d(Shape)
rm1 = Color is Green ; Color is Green?
notrun = rm3
rm3 = Color is Red ; Color is Red?

running = Green - d(shape) - Red

Shape	**Red**	**Green**	**-d(shape)**	**running**
0	0	0		0
1	0	1	-1	0
2	0	2	-1	1
3	1	0	-1	-2
3	1	1	0	0
2	1	2	1	0
1	2	0	1	1
0	2	1	1	1

2. A6 gets legs

Let us crawl on land and get legs and start walking. Keep the A5 Robot but remove the rudder, propeller, sensors and brain. We do not have balance yet, so let us start with a four legged Robot. We will hinge the legs on the four corners of the A5 body. Four legged travel is harder than two legged travel but we can do it without balance sensors.

A6 = {eyes, legs}
 legs = {foot/ankle, knee, hip} ; three hinges with servos.
  foot/ankle = {faLF, faRF, faLR, faRR}
  knee = {knLF, knRF, knLR, knRR}
  hip = {hiLF, hiRF, hiLR, hiRR}

eyes = {eyeL, eyeR}; Buy two Eyevhx from Hal Brain Design.

Goals = {seek objects}
Actions {walk, steer}

dIntensity = IntensityL - IntensityR ; from eyes.
Size = LengthL + HeightL ; get size from L and H.
dir = dIntensity ; to steer by

walking = n(d(Size)) - Pain ; We chase size as ;before.

Starting with front legs. I flounder along. Here I am working from a sort of truth table to equations rather than the other way around. I do not have a four legged animal to copy, but I have two legs to start the front. Here is what happens when I step.

step left

LF	RF
1.hip bends,	1.ankle bends
2.knee bends,	2.hip unbends
3.ankle unbends	3.knee unbends
4.knee unbends	

step right

LF	RF
1.ankle bends	1.hip bends
2.hip unbends	2.knee bends
3.knee unbends	3.ankle unbends
	4.knee unbends

walking is step left then step right
stepping left is:
{hiLFBending, n(faLFBending), faRFBending, n(hiRFBending)}
stepping right is:
{hiRFBending, n(faRFBending), faLFBending, n(hiLFBending)}

```
SteppingLF = hiLFBending o ltm1
 ltm1 = ltm2 o faRFBending
  ltm2 = n(faLFBending) o n(hiRFBending) ;n is negative of()

SteppingRF = hiRFBending o rtm1
 rtm1 = rtm2 o faLFBending
  rtm2 = n(faRFBending) o n(hiLFBending)

Left front
hip
hiLFBending = hiLFBend - hiLFNotBend
 hiLFBend = stepLF + hiLFPainl
 hiLFNotBend = stepRF + hiLFPainh
  hiLFPainh = hiLFBending > hiLimith
  hiLFPainl = hiLGBending < hiLimitl
ankle
faLFBending = faLFBend - faLFNotBend
 faLFBend = stepRF + faLFPainl
 faLFNotBend = stepLF + faLFPainh
  faLFPainh = faLFBending > faLimith
```

faLFPainl = faLFBending < faLimitl

knee

knLFBending = knLFBend - knLFNotBend

knLFBend = d(hiLFBending) + knLFPainl

knLFNotBend = knLFPainh

knLFPainh = knLFBending > knLimitp

knLFPainl = knLFBending < knLimitl

Bends with hip and zeros when hip stops.

Right front

hips

```
hiRFBending = hiRFBend - hiRFNotBend
 hiRFBend = stepRF + hiRFPainl
 hiRFNotBend = stepLF + hiRFPainh
  hiRFPainh = hiRFBending > hiLimith
  hiRFPainl = hiRGBending < hiLimitl
```

ankle

```
faRFBending = faRFBend - faRFNotBend
 faRFBend = stepLF + faRFPainl
 faRFNotBend = stepRF + faRFPainh
  faRFPainh = faRFBending > faLimith
  faRFPainl = faRFBending < faLimitl
```

knee

```
knRFBending = knRFBend - knRFNotBend
 knRFBend = d(hiRFBending) + knRFPainl
 knRFNotBend = knRFPainh
  knRFPainh = knRFBending > knLimitp
  knRFPainl = knRFBending < knLimitl
```

Step functions

```
stepLF = tLF if done(steppingRF)
 tLF = walking - dir
stepRF = tRF if done(steppingLF)
 tRF = walking + dir
```

Change +,- dir to change direction to suite. + is right here and - is left.

Here is a truth table of step:

walk	dir	d(Le)	d(RI)	stepRF	stepLF	
0	0	0	0	0	0	
4	0	1	0	0	4	
4	1	0	1	5	0	turn right
4	1	1	0	0	3	
4	1	0	1	5	0	
4	1	1	0	0	3	
4	0	0	1	4	0	
4	-1	1	0	0	1	
4	-1	0	1	3	0	turn left
4	-1	1	0	0	5	
4	-1	0	1	3	0	
4	-1	1	0	0	5	

We are depending on leg motion to stop before cycling. I do not know what will happen if legs are forced.

Rear legs do not steer, which makes coding a lot easier. I collect stepping from the rear legs, separately from the front legs. Rear legs can be coupled to front by using front StepLF and StepRF in the rear or they can be decoupled by providing separate StepR and StepL functions. That is what is done here.

If we couple front and rear, this code can be eliminated.

```
SteppingLR = hiLRBending o lrtm1
lrtm1 = lrtm2 o faRRBending
lrtm2 = n(faLRBending) o n(hiRRBending)

SteppingRR = hiRRBending o rrtm1
rrtm1 = rrtm2 o faLRBending
rrtm2 = n(faRRBending) o n(hiLRBending)
```

This code is for either system from now on.

Left rear

hip

```
hiLRBending = hiLRBend - hiLRNotBend
 hiLRBend = stepLR + hiLRPainl
 hiLRNotBend = stepRR + hiLRPainh
  hiLRPainh = hiLRBending > hiLimith
  hiLRPainl = hiLRBending < hiLimitl
```

ankle

```
faLRBending = faLRBend - faLRNotBend
 faLRBend = stepRR + faLRPainl
 faLRNotBend = stepLR + faLRPainh
  faLRPainh = faLRBending > faLimith
  faLRPainl = faLRBending < faLimitl
```

knee

```
knLRBending = knLRBend - knLRNotBend
 knLRBend = d(hiLRBending) + knLRPainl
 knLRNotBend = knLRPainh
  knLRPainh = knLRBending > knLimith
  knLRPainl = knLrBending < knLimitl
```

Right rear
hip

```
hiRRBending = hiRRBend - hiRRNotBend
 hiRRBend = stepRR + hiRRPainl
 hiRRNotBend = stepLR + hiRRPainh
  hiRRPainh = hiRRBending > hiLimith
  hiRRPainl = hiRRBending < hiLimitl
```

ankle

```
faRRBending = faRRBend - faRRNotBend
 faRRBend = stepLR + faRRPainl
 faRRNotBend = stepRR + faRRPainh
  faRRPainh = faRRBending > faLimith
  faRRPainl = faRRBending < faLimitl
```

knee

```
knRRBending = knRRBend - knRRNotBend
 knRRBend = d(hiRRBending) + knRRPainl
 knRRNotBend = knRRPainh
  knRRPainh = knRRBending > knLimith
  knRRPainl = knRRBending < knLimitl

stepRR = walk if done(steppingLF)
stepLR = walk if done(steppingLR)
```

Here following is a perfect example of collecting data going down the tree. Note the variable name changes as we go down.

```
;Collect pain for hips, LF, RF, LR, RR
;left
 hiLPainh = hiLFPainh o hiLRPainh ; left hip
;pain high
```

```
 hiLPainl = hiLFPainl o hiLRPainl ; left hip
;pain low
hiLPain = hiLPainh o hiLPainl    ; left hip
;pain
;right
 hiRPainh = hiRFPainh o hiRRPainh ; right hip
;pain high
 hiRPainl = hiRFPainl o hiRRPainl ; right hip
;pain low
hiRPain = hiRPainh o hiRPainl     ; right hip
;pain
;
hiPain = hiLPain o hiRPain        ; hip pain
```

;Collect pain for ankles

;left
faLPainh = faLFPainh o faLRPainh ; left ankle pain high
faLPainl = faLFPainl o faLRPainl ; left ankle ;pain low
faLPain = faLPainh o faLPainl ; left ankle ;pain

;right

faRPainh = faRFPainh o faRRPainh ; right ankle pain high
faRPainl = faRFPainl o faRRPainl ; right ankle pain low
faRPain = faRPainh o faRPainl ; right ankle pain
;
faPain = faLPain o faRPain ; ankle pain
;Collect pain for knees
;left
knLPainh = knLFPainh o knLRPainh ; left knee ;pain high
knLPainl = knLFPainl o knLRPainl ; left knee ;pain low
knLPain = knLPainh o knLPainl ; left knee ;pain
;right

```
 knRPainh = knRFPainh o knRRPainh ; right knee
;pain high
 knRPainl = knRFPainl o knRRPainl ; right knee
;pain low
knRPain = knRPainh o knRPainl     ; right knee
;pain
;
knPain = knLPain o knRPain          ; knee pain
;
LPain = LPm1 + hiLPain          ;Left pain
 LPm1 = knLPain + faLPain
RPain = RPm1 + hiRPain          ;Right pain
 RPm1 = knRPain + faRPain
;
Pain = LPain + RPain            ;All pain
```

This is simplified as much as I can. There is only one gait although there are 256 speeds and the front and rear are not coupled in any way. Each has its own step function, like a centipede.

This Robot can be extended to a centipede by duplicating the rear legs another ninety eight times.

Walk is not yet defined. We can make it chase some eye function as we did before. While debugging, we can always make walk a constant with a number pad before we connect the real sensors.

Now let us write it up as a program. I have rearranged some of the code for neatness. Actual order, of course makes no difference at all to the Robot, since all this is going on at the same time. It is delimited so a computer could read this file without trouble.

2. A6 Program

```
A6.ani ; a four legged walking Robot
Author: Harold L. Reed
Copyright 2009 Harold L. Reed
;A6 = {eyes, legs}
; legs = {foot/ankle, knee, hip} ; three
hinges with servos.
; foot/ankle = {faLF, faRF, faLR, faRR}
; knee = {knLF, knRF, knLR, knRR}
; hip = {hiLF, hiRF, hiLR, hiRR}
;Knee bends while hip is bending.
; eyes = {eyeL, eyeR} ; borrow the eyes from
A5
;Goals = {seek objects}
;Actions {walk, steer}
Length = LengthL o LengthR ; from eyes.
dLength = LengthL - LengthR
Height = HeightL o HeightR
Size = Length + Height ; we use what we need
;from eye.
;Set limits of travel before pain occurs.
hiLimith = 100
hiLimitl = -100
knLimith = 50
knLimitl = -5
faLimith = 10
faLimitl = -5

;Collect pain for hips, LF, RF, LR, RR
;left
hiLPainh = hiLFPainh o hiLRPainh ; left hip
;pain high
hiLPainl = hiLFPainl o hiLRPainl ; left hip
;pain low
hiLPain = hiLPainh o hiLPainl    ; left hip
;pain
```

```
;right
hiRPainh = hiRFPainh o hiRRPainh ; right hip
;pain high
hiRPainl = hiRFPainl o hiRRPainl ; right hip
;pain low
hiRPain = hiRPainh o hiRPainl    ; right hip
;pain
;
hiPain = hiLPain o hiRPain      ; hip pain
;
;Collect pain for ankles
;left
faLPainh = faLFPainh o faLRPainh ; left ankle
;pain high
faLPainl = faLFPainl o faLRPainl ; left ankle
;pain low
faLPain = faLPainh o faLPainl    ; left ankle
;pain
;right
faRPainh = faRFPainh o faRRPainh ; right ankle
;pain high
faRPainl = faRFPainl o faRRPainl ; right ankle
;pain low
faRPain = faRPainh o faRPainl    ; right ankle
;pain
;
```

```
faPain = faLPain o faRPain          ; ankle pain
;Collect pain for knees
;left
knLPainh = knLFPainh o knLRPainh ; left knee
;pain high
knLPainl = knLFPainl o knLRPainl ; left knee
;pain low
knLPain = knLPainh o knLPainl      ; left knee
;pain
;right
knRPainh = knRFPainh o knRRPainh ; right knee
;pain high
knRPainl = knRFPainl o knRRPainl ; right knee
;pain low
knRPain = knRPainh o knRPainl      ; right knee
;pain
;
knPain = knLPain o knRPain          ; knee pain
;
LPain = LPm1 + hiLPain          ;Left pain
LPm1 = knLPain + faLPain
RPain = RPm1 + hiRPain          ;Right pain
RPm1 = knRPain + faRPain
;
Pain = LPain + RPain            ;All pain
;
;collect status
LFStatus = LFm1 + hiLFBending
LFm1 = knLFBending + faLFBending

steering = turnL - turnR
turnL = LengthL + RPain ; to steer by
turnR = LengthR + LPain
walking = walk - nowalk
walk = n(d(Size))
nowalk = Pain ; We chase the rate of change of
;size
```

```
; as before. Walking also affects the Size change, so this
; should be checked.

;------------ FRONT ---------------
;Left front
;hip
hiLFBending = hiLFBend - hiLFNotBend
 hiLFBend = stepLF + hiLFPainl
 hiLFNotBend = stepRF + hiLFPainh
  hiLFPainh = hiLFBending > hiLimith
  hiLFPainl = hiLGBending < hiLimitl
;ankle
faRFBending = faRFBend - faRFNotBend
 faRFBend = stepLF + faRFPainl
 faRFNotBend = stepRF + faRFPainh
  faRFPainh = faRFBending > faLimith
  faRFPainl = faRFBending < faLimitl
;knee
knRFBending = knRFBend - knRFNotBend
 knRFBend = d(hiRFBending) + knRFPainl
 knRFNotBend = knRFPainh
  knRFPainh = knRFBending > knLimitp
  knRFPainl = knRFBending < knLimitl
;Right front
;
;hips
hiRFBending = hiRFBend - hiRFNotBend
 hiRFBend = stepRF + hiRFPainl
 hiRFNotBend = stepLF + hiRFPainh
  hiRFPainh = hiRFBending > hiLimith
  hiRFPainl = hiRGBending < hiLimitl
;ankle
faRFBending = faRFBend - faRFNotBend
faRFBend = stepLF + faRFPainl
faRFNotBend = stepRF + faRFPainh
faRFPainh = faRFBending > faLimith
faRFPainl = faRFBending < faLimitl
```

```
;knee
knRFBending = knRFBend - knRFNotBend
knRFBend = d(hiRFBending) + knRFPainl
knRFNotBend = knRFPainh
knRFPainh = knRFBending > knLimitp
knRFPainl = knRFBending < knLimitl
;
; step functions
stepLF = tLF if done(steppingRF)
 tLF = walking - steering

stepRF = tRF if done(steppingLF)
 tRF = walking + steering
; step status
SteppingLF = hiLFBending o ltm1
 ltm1 = ltm2 o faRFBending
  ltm2 = n(faLFBending) o n(hiRFBending);n is
;negative of ()
SteppingRF = hiRFBending o rtm1
 rtm1 = rtm2 o faLFBending
  rtm2 = n(faRFBending) o n(hiLFBending)
```

```
; ----------- REAR -----------
;Left rear
;hip
hiLRBending = hiLRBend - hiLRNotBend
 hiLRBend = stepLR + hiLRPainl
 hiLRNotBend = stepRR + hiLRPainh
  hiLRPainh = hiLRBending > hiLimith
  hiLRPainl = hiLRBending < hiLimitl
;ankle
faLRBending = faLRBend - faLRNotBend
 faLRBend = stepRR + faLRPainl
 faLRNotBend = stepLR + faLRPainh
  faLRPainh = faLRBending > faLimith
  faLRPainl = faLRBending < faLimitl
;knee
knLRBending = knLRBend - knLRNotBend
 knLRBend = d(hiLRBending) + knLRPainl
 knLRNotBend = knLRPainh
  knLRPainh = knLRBending > knLimith
  knLRPainl = knLrBending < knLimitl

;Right rear
;hip
hiRRBending = hiRRBend - hiRRNotBend
 hiRRBend = stepRR + hiRRPainl
 hiRRNotBend = stepLR + hiRRPainh
  hiRRPainh = hiRRBending > hiLimith
  hiRRPainl = hiRRBending < hiLimitl
;ankle
faRRBending = faRRBend - faRRNotBend
 faRRBend = stepLR + faRRPainl
 faRRNotBend = stepRR + faRRPainh
  faRRPainh = faRRBending > faLimith
  faRRPainl = faRRBending < faLimitl
;knee
knRRBending = knRRBend - knRRNotBend
 knRRBend = d(hiRRBending) + knRRPainl
 knRRNotBend = knRRPainh
  knRRPainh = knRRBending > knLimith
  knRRPainl = knRRBending < knLimitl
```

```
; step function rear
stepRR = d(steppingRR) z walking
stepLR = d(steppingLR) z walking
; step status rear
SteppingLR = hiLRBending o lrtm1
 lrtm1 = lrtm2 o faRRBending
  lrtm2 = n(faLRBending) o n(hiRRBending)
;
SteppingRR = hiRRBending o rrtm1
 rrtm1 = rrtm2 o faLRBending
  rrtm2 = n(faRRBending) o n(hiLRBending)
END A6
```

1. A Big Robot - Big Al

Robots go across disciplines, so here I will make a general purpose, human sized robot that we can all study and add to.

The purpose here is to build the equations for a man sized model robot. I will follow the structure of a human being, but will simplify when possible. Where humans may have millions of sensors, I can get by with one or two. Our replica will be crude and lumpy, but it should function like the original as a good model should.

For power, I will assume a fuel cell. The robot should drink gasoline. That means it must breathe, exhale, drink and pee.

There will be many variables, so I need some order here. The big body parts provide a division. I need a fixed viewpoint for left and right and front and back, since we are somewhat symmetrical. Our viewpoint is from the robot's perspective. Looking over the robot head, in the direction of the eyes, Left is left, front is front.

The main objects and actions are:

Key Objects	Actions
He Head	Holds eyes,ears, nose, mouth and brain
er Ears (LR)	Sound levels, frequency
ey eyes(LR)	light levels, objects
no nose	inhales, exhales
mo mouth	exhales, makes sound, drinks
Ne Neck	turns head
Sh Shoulders(LR)	holds neck and arms
Ar Arms(LR)	hinges at shoulder
el elbows(LR)	bend
wr wrists(LR)	bend
ha hands(LR)	clasp
fi fingers(5 LR)	bend
To Torso	holds shoulders, hips and power

hi hips(LR) hold legs
le legs(LR) hinges at hip
kn knees(LR) bend
an ankles(LR) bend
fe feet(LR) support

Variables will be prefixed with the symbol for the structure. If I make other structures inside, I will use the structure prefix and a minor structure prefix. L or R indicating left or right will follow that. F and B will represent front and back.

Types of physical sensors are:

Symbol	Sensor type
L	Light (Light intensity)
S	Sound (In air)
P	Pressure (sound in other media)
T	Temperature

Types of physical motors are:

Symbol	Motor type
R	Motor producing rotating motion
B	Motor producing bending motion
S	Motor producing sound
P	Pumps
V	Valves

For intermediate HalStreams, I will use the symbol M with a column, row suffix.

These equations are written in sequence, but I say again, to remember that all these equations are active all the time, so the order in which they are written is meaningless. And remember that these equations represent hardware. The variables are cables and the operators are HalNodes.

Since there is a lot of comment here along with the actual Robot equations, the equations alone will be in **bold** text.

I start at the bottom, doing the easy parts first. The first thing to do is to set up the motors. Then I go back and set up all the sensors. Then I add brain and improvements. I must learn for our Robot, but that I can do easily. It can't reproduce either, but I can build it. Robot design is an iterative process that is very much like designing a computer program but much easier. There is no sequence to worry about. Every function can be worked on by a separate crew. The equations will outlive the Robot and go toward making the next. Evolution here works by standardization and communication. (Mistakes that work will change the code for the next Robot.)

Like a computer program, I write the code, which relates the variables to the actions, and then I assemble the HalNodes and cables to build the Robot. Assembly is done in several steps and can be done for each function/motor separately.

1. Gather the HalNodes and place them in the Robot or layout.
2. Count the plugs for each cable variable.
3. Assemble the cables by placing the plugs on them to match HalNode sockets for each function. Provide an extra plug for power on each motor variable.

Since BigAl is a large project, tree notation is used, so intermediate variables are not always shown.

2. Feet

The (left and right feet are mirror images of each other. I do the left one and copy for the right one.)
Foot is hinged at the ankle. The normal angle is about 90 degrees and the travel is about 10 degrees plus or minus. The rotation is counter clockwise looking from the right side. The instruction to bend comes from down the leg and from the foot. It hurts to bend too far. The motor that produces the ankle bend can be some kind of servo, where the bend Hal stream produces an angle change. It is in the actual process of building this Robot that such things need to be considered. The brain design indicates what is needed. Engineering provides the how to do it.

I need some sensors in the foot. Let us put a couple of pressure sensors fore and aft on the bottom.
fePLF and fePLB are the pressure HalStreams going up the leg.
feBendL is the Hal stream coming down the leg.
fePT is the pain threshold, coming down the leg.
fePainL is the pain Hal stream going up the leg.

feBendingL = feDoBendL - feNoBendL
 feDoBendL = stepR o fePainlL o fePLF

feNoBendL = stepL o fePainL o fePLB o default
; pain collection
fePainhL = feBendingL > feLimith
fePainlL = feBending < feLimitl

feet and ankle have 3 sensors and 1 motor.

For the right foot and ankle do the same but rename the variables.

```
feBendingR = feDoBendR - feNoBendR
 feDoBendR = stepL o fePRF o fePainRl
 feNoBendR = stepR o fePRB o fePainR o default
 fePainhR = feBendingR > feLimith
 fePainlR = feBendingR < feLimitl
```

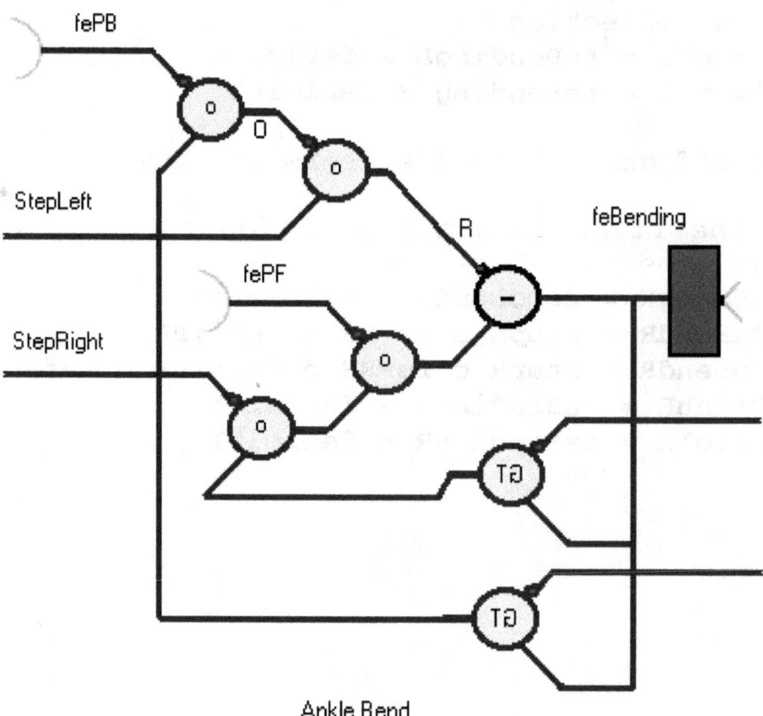

Figure 14 Ankle motor

2. Knees

Symbol kn.
Knees bend. Resting angle is about 0. Bend max is about -270 degrees. There are two knees, left and right and they are symmetrical. The rotation is clockwise from the right side.

Left knee:

```
knBendingL = knBend - knDon'tBendL
 knBendL = d(hiBendingL) o Sit o knPainlL
 knDon'tBendL = Stand o knPainhL o default
; pain collection tree
 knPainhL = knBending > knLimith
 knPainlL = knBending < knLimitl
```

Right knee:

```
knBendingR = knBendR  - knDon'tBendR
 knBendR = d(hiBendingR) o Sit o knPainlR
 knDon'tBendR = Stand o knPainR o default
; Pain collection tree
 knPainhR = knBendingR > knLimith
 knPainlR = knBendingR < knLimitl
```

2. Hips

Symbol hi.
Two hips, left and right. Hinge angle is 0 degrees to 270. The rotation is counter clockwise looking from the right side.

Left hip:

```
hiBendingL = hiBendL - hinotbendL
 hiBendL = stepL o Sit o hiPainlL
 hinotbendL=stepR o Stand o hiPainL o default
 hiPainhL = hiBendingL > hiLimith
 hiPainlL = hiBendingL < hiLimitl
```

;Right hip:

```
hiBendingR = hiBendR - hinotbendR
```

```
hiBendR = stepR o Sit o hiPainlR
hinotbendR=stepL o Stand o hiPainR o default
hiPainhR = hiBendingR > PainThresholdh
hiPainlR = hiBendingR < PainThresholdl
```

I am attaching some pressure or touch sensors to each hip back so Big Al can tell when it is sitting.

```
hiPL and hiPR
dhiP = hiPL - hiPR ; difference in pressure
hiP = hiPL + hiPR
```

Sitting and Standing

```
sitting = sit - nosit
 sit = IsStanding ;{have place to sit}
 nosit = hiPain

sat = sitting z satcode

IsSitting = hiP
```

Sit and stand are opposites. When sitting knees are bent, hips are bent, ankles are straight. To sit, both knees bend and both hips bend. To stand, both knees unbend and both hips unbend. Ankles keep flat. Of course you cannot sit unless you are standing and you cannot stand unless you are sitting.

```
standing = stand - nostand
 stand = IsSitting ;{all the things needing
;standing}
 nostand = knPain

stood = standing z stoodcode

IsStanding = Not(hiP)
```

3. Walking

```
walking = walk - nowalk  ; When to walk
 walk = stood + {All the things causing walk}
 nowalk = Peeing o Drinking o AnyPain

walked = walking z wcode
```

step left

L	R
1.hip bends,	1.ankle bends
2.knee bends,	2.hip unbends
3.ankle unbends	3.knee unbends
4.knee unbends	

step right

L	R
1.ankle bends	1.hip bends
2.hip unbends	2.knee bends
3.knee unbends	3.ankle unbends
	4.knee unbends

walking is step left then step right
stepping left is:
{hiBendingL, n(feBendingL), feBendingR, n(hiBendingR)}
stepping right is:
{hiBendingR, n(feBendingR), feBendingL, n(hiBendingL)}

```
IsSteppingL = hiBendingL o feBendingR o
n(feBendingL) o n(hiBendingR)

IsSteppingR = hiBendingR o feBendingL o
n(feBendingR) o n(hiBendingL)
```

Step functions

```
stepL = d(IsSteppingR) z walking - dir
stepR = d(IsSteppingL) z walking + dir
```

Change +,- dir to change direction to suite. + is to the right here and - is to the left.

Torso

Torso is the structure that holds the hips and shoulders. In our model, it will contain the fuel cell. It will need to contain fuel, methane or whatever, and water. It will need to input and hold air for the oxygen. If gasoline is the fuel, then CO_2 is also emitted.

(Fuel cell is: 2e = 2H + O; Strip the electron off two hydrogen atoms, introduce an oxygen molecule and you produce water and have two electrons for the electricity.)

It will need a bladder of some sort to hold the water. It may need a pump from the fuel cell. I doubt that it can work under pressure. It will need a tube from the water bladder to empty it occasionally. It will need a valve on that tube. It will need a pressure sensor to indicate how the fullness of the bladder. Since these functions are singular, I can leave off prefix names. I do have two bladders, water and fuel.

Water pressure sensor is WaterPressure

Peeing = WaterPressure > Don'tPee ; Valve is ;on or off.

Don'tPee = fePainL o fePainR o Drinking o **walk o default** ; Add other inhibitors as needed.

Don'tPee is the tree of all inhibitors. I can define these later and add or take away functions at will. The point is that I can establish a goal and an anti goal without knowing at this time what they are. I have also used functions that will be defined later in this program.

The fuel bladder is almost the opposite of the water bladder. Now I have a tube/funnel input mechanism so the Robot can drink. Again, I measure pressure on the bladder. The need for fuel is felt by low pressure in the fuel bladder.

The motor here is a valve and pump. The goal is to drink.

Drinking = drink - FuelPressure ; Drink until ;full. It can drink whenever it has something ;to drink.

The fuel is fed to a preprocessor that strips off the hydrogen, leaving us with carbon dioxide and other junk.
I need a pump to exhaust this into the air. This is part of breathing, but I will not control it now. I will simply pump it out all the time. Our Robot may have bad breath.
I need a pump to put air into another bladder, toA .

Breathing = breathe - toAP ; breathe until full. ;
breathe could be constant

Now I have power for everything. Remember that Hal stream cables also carry the power for the HalNodes, motors and sensors.

2. Shoulders

Shoulders carry the neck and the arms. I am back to left and right. Neck is at the center and arms are at the left and right edges. Arms are attached to the shoulder with both hinges and rotary connections. Arms can rotate on the shoulder and they are hinged to swing outward from the shoulder. I can use a screw device to lever the arm(s) outward. That motor, in turn revolves around a shaft that rotates in a bearing in the shoulder. The arm is

attached to the shaft. The shaft rotates the arm and the hinge.
The shaft motor is arR left or right. The hinge motor is arH left or right. There are touch sensors under each arm. arPL and arPR.

Left arm:

```
arRotatingL = arRotateL - arNotRotateL
 arRotateL = walking o FATilting o arPainlL
 arNotRotateL = arRotPainhL + default
  arRotPainhL = arRotatingL > arRotLimith
  arRotPainlL = arRotatingL < arRotLimitl
; Lifting
arLiftingL = arLiftL - arNotLiftL
 arLiftL = LRTilting
  arNotLiftL = arLiftPainhL + default + arPL
  arLiftPAinhL = arLifting > arLiftLimith
```

Right arm:

```
;Rotating
arRotatingR = arRotateR - arNotRotateR
 arRotateR = walking o FATilting o arRotPainlR
 arNotRotateR = arRotPainhR + default
  arRotPainhR = arRotatingR > arRotLimith
  arRotPainlR = arRotatingR < arRotLimitl

; Lifting
arLiftingR = arLiftR - arNotLiftR
 arLiftR = n(LRTilting);change if reversed
 arNotLiftR = arLiftPainhR + default + arPR
  arLiftPainhR = arLiftingR > arLiftLimith
```

I have motors to lift and swing the arms. Four motors total.

2. Elbows

The elbow is a simple hinge. It is straight at 0 degrees and bends forward as much as it can.

Left:

```
;Left:
elBendingL = elBendL - elDon'tBendL
 elBendL = elPainlL
 elDon'tBendL = elPainhL + default
  elPainhL = elBendingL > elLimith
  elPainlL = elBendingL < elLimitl
```

Right:

```
elBendingR = elBendR - elDon'tBendR
 elBendR = elPainlR
 elDon'tBendR = elPainhR + default
  elPainhR = elBendingR > elLimith
  elPainlR = elBendingR < elLimitl
;Two motors.
```

2. Wrist

The wrist flops back and forth.

Left:

```
wrBendingL = wrBendL - wrDon'tBendL
 wrBendL = wrPainlL
 wrDon'tBendL = wrPainhL + default
  wrPainhL = wrBendingL > wrLimith
  wrPainlL = wrBendingL < wrLimitl
```

Right:

```
wrBendingR = wrBendR - wrDon'tBendR
 wrBendR = wrPainlR
 wrDon'tBendR = wrPainhR + default
  wrPainhR = wrBending > wrLimith
  wrPainlR = wrBending < wrLimitl
;Two motors
```

2. Fingers

There are 4 fingers and a thumb on each hand. (I just counted them.) From the thumb th, number them: in is index, mi is middle, ri is ring and li is little. Each finger has 3 hinges. Number them from the hand, h1, h2, h3.

Each finger has two motors, one motor on hinge h1 and one motor on hinge h2. The motor on hinge h2 also bends the hinge h3. I cannot bend hinge h3 by itself unless I physically suppress the bending of hinge h2. (I am the only example of a human being around as I write this.)

The thumb has two hinges and two motors. There is another hinge and motor that rotates the thumb under the hand.

mf1h1 is the motor on the first hinge of the first finger.

The major operation of the hand is to clasp something. It also touches things. The ha-ClaspL and haDon'tClaspL Hal stream comes down the arm. Also hand clasping is inhibited on each finger by touch.

```
haToClaspingL = haClaspL - haNotClaspL
 haClaspL = {}
 haNotClaspL = default
 inh1BendingL = haToClaspingL - inPL
 inh2BendingL = haToClaspingL - inPL
 inh3BendingL = inh2BendingL
 mih1BendingL = haToClaspingL - miPL
 mih2BendingL = haToClaspingL - miPL
 mih3BendingL = mih2BendingL
 rih1BendingL = haToClaspingL - riPL
 rih2BendingL = haToClaspingL - riPL
 rih3BendingL = rih2BendingL
 lih1BendingL = haToClaspingL - liPL
 lih2BendingL = haToClaspingL - liPL
 lih3BendingL = lih2BendingL
```

Now the thumb. For now, leave out the rotation.

```
 th2BendingL = haToClaspingL - thPL
 th3BendingL = haToClaspingL - thPL
```

This is a good example of how a master command or goal gets split into sub goals and tasks.

Now lets repeat this for the right hand.

```
haToClaspingR = haClaspR - haNotClaspR
 haClaspR = {}
 haNotClaspR = default
 inh1BendingR = haToClaspingR - inPR
 inh2BendingR = haToClaspingR - inPR
 inh3BendingR = inh2BendingR
 mih1BendingR = haToClaspingR - miPR
 mih2BendingR = haToClaspingR - miPR
 mih3BendingR = mih2BendingR
 rih1BendingR = haToClaspingR - riPR
 rih2BendingR = haToClaspingR - riPR
 rih3BendingR = rih2BendingR
 lih1BendingR = haToClaspingR - liPR
 lih2BendingR = haToClaspingR - liPR
 lih3BendingR = lih2BendingR
```

Now the right thumb.

```
 th2BendingR = haToClaspingR - thPR
 th3BendingR = haToClaspingR - thPR
```

28 motors total.

```
; Collect left hand touches
;
dliriL = liPL - riPL ; little - ring
dmiinL = miPL - riPL ; middle - ring
dinmiL = inPL - miPL ; index - middle
;
slL = drimiL + dliriL ; sum left side
srL = dmiinL + drimiL ; sum right side

sL = srL + slL        ; sum all
;
TouchingriliL = dliriL z 1 ;ring + little
TouchinglimiinL = srL z 2;little+middle+index
TouchingAllL = sl z 5    ;all
TouchingrimiL = dinmiL z 3 ;index + middle
TouchingrimiinL = slL z 4 ;index+Middle+ring
;
O1or2L = TouchingriliL o TouchingmiriliL
```

```
O1or20r5L = O1or2L o touchingAllL
O3or4L = TouchinginmiL o TouchinginmiriL
OAllL = O1or2or5L o O3or4L
```

```
; Collect right hand touches
;
driliR = riPR - liPR ; ring - little
dmiriR = liPR - riPR ; middle - ring
dinmiR = inPR - miPR ; index - middle
;
srR = driliR + dmiriR ; sum of differences
slR = dinmiR + dmiriR
sR = slR + srR            ;sum of sum
;
TouchingriliR = driliR z 1 ;ring = little
TouchingmiriliR = srR z 2 ;middle=ring=little
TouchingAllR = sR z 5    ;all fingers
TouchinginmiR = dinmiR z 3 ;index = middle
TouchinginmiriR = slR z 4 ;index=middle=ring
;
O1or2R = TouchingriliR o TouchingmiriliR
O1or2Or5R = O1or2R o touchingAllR
O3or4R = TouchinginmiR o TouchinginmiriR
OAllR = O1or2or5R o O3or4R

haTouching = OAllR o OAllL
haTouched = Touching z hatouchedcode
```

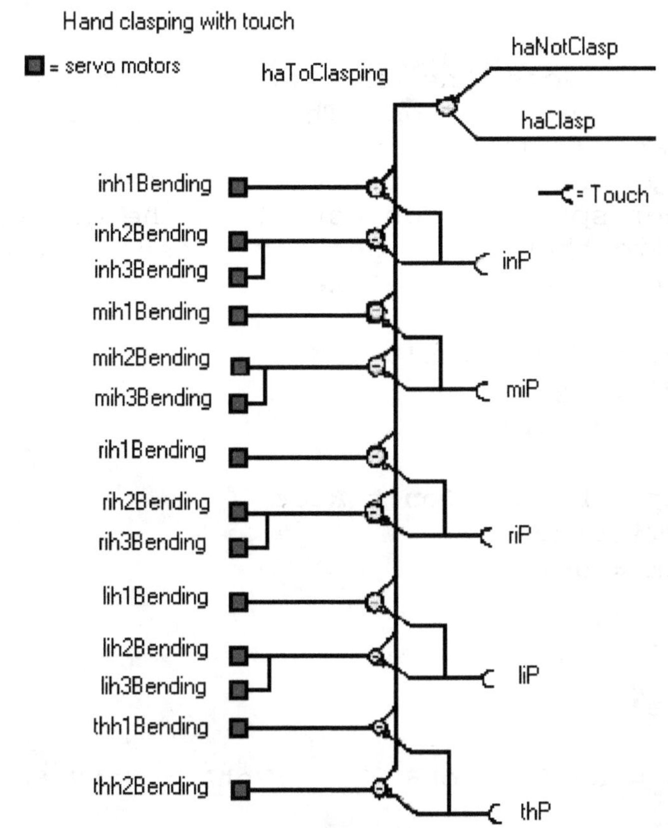

Figure 15 Hand Clasping

2. Neck

Neck connects the shoulder to the head and controls head motion. The head can turn, nod back and forth and rock right and left. Fortunately, the motors for the neck can go in the shoulder space. I can establish the motors quickly. Now that I am getting close to the head, I can leave off prefixes.

HeadNodding = Nod - Don't nod
 Nod = FATilting
 Don't nod = default

HeadRocking = Rock - Don't Rock
 Rock = LRTilting
 Don't Rock = default

Two motors.

Head Rotate

HeadRotate = RotL - RotR ;RotL > RotR Rotate left
 RotL = IntensityL + LoudnessL + RotPainR
 RotR = IntensityR + LoudnessR + RotPainL
  RotPainL = HeadRotate > HRLimitL
  RotPAinR = HeadRotate < HRLimitR
; Add the ears, look at light or sound.
Dir = HeadRotate ; follow the eyes.
One motor.

2. Head

The head holds the minor motors for eye movement and sound but it is mostly full of sensors. Eyes, ears and balance are the main ones. I simplify like crazy here.

Speaking = Speak - Don't Speak
 Speak = {Pain}
 Don’t Speak = drinking o default

Smiling = smile - frown
 smile = default + Goodness
 frown = anyPain

Two motors.

I now have all the motors of the Robot established. Other than a few sensors in the foot, I have no sensors yet. If I power up the Robot now, it will flop around "like a chicken with its head cut off." (The latches in my HalNodes are CMOS and tend to emit random integers when they have no input.) Sensors and brain HalNodes complete the loop and I am at that point now. Every undefined cable must be connected to something.

Balance

The first sensors in the head are for balance. I need a sensor that provides an integer for fore and aft and right and left tilt. Let positive numbers indicate forward and right tilt and negative numbers indicate backward and left tilt. Of course, zero is no tilt. Sensor names are: FATilt and RLTilt for fore and aft and right and left respectively. Animals have two of each. So can I: FATiltL and FATiltR for fore and aft and LRTiltL and LRTiltR. Now, as nature does, I can eliminate absolutes, knock out differences and clean up our inputs.

FATilting = FATiltF - FATiltA ; the differences
LRTilting = LRTiltL - LRTiltR ;
The balance goal is to keep FATilting and LRTilting close to zero.

Since this is our mechanical man we can equip it with any instruments we want. It could have a radio link. It could have a GPS system for global position reference. Robot evolution can be much faster than our biological evolution. When we learn how language works and how to read, so can they. So, how do we keep Robots from building Robots. They can read the instructions, too. We need to think about that now.

3. Ears

Buy two Ear1.ani from Hal Brain Design. Call them EarR and EarL

Loudness = LoudnessL o LoudnessR
dLoudness = LoudnessL - LoundnessR ; sound direction
dLoud = dLoudL o dLoudR

Sound = Loudness + dLoud
IsSound = Sound > 0
WasSound = Sound z WasSoundCode

3. Eyes

I will use the eyes developed in the vision chapter. They will be EyeL and EyeR. From them will come:
LengthL and LengthR, HeightL and HeightR, ColorsL and ColorsR for each object detected. We derive:

Length = LengthL o LengthR
Height = HeightL o HeightR

Shape = Length - Height ; Shape code
Size = Length + Height ; size code

;and
dShape = ShapeL - ShapeR ;3d shape code
dSize = SizeL - SizeR

Object = Shape + Size

ObjectSeeing = Object + Color + Sound + ha-Touch

ObjectSeen = ObjectSeeing z ObjectSeenCode
Color = ColorL o ColorR

3. Constants

Legs

```
feLimith = 100
feLimitl = -10
knLimith = 200
knLimitL = -1
hiLimith = 200
hiLimitl = -2
```

Arms

```
arRotLimith = 200
arRotLimitl = -200
arLiftLimith = 200
wrLimith = 100
wrLimitl = -100
```

Head

```
HRLimitL = 100
HRLimitR = -100
```

Global

```
default = 10
```

3. Codes

```
smilecode = 10
walkedcode = 11
peedcode = 12
stoodcode = 13
satcode = 14
WasSoundCode = 15
ObjectSeenCode = 16
wasobject = 17
hatouchedcode = 18
```

3. Emotions

Now I must pay attention to the internal state and to the goals of this Robot. I would like to see how it feels, so I can make motors to show emotion.

Goodness = Good - Bad
 Good = WhatDone
 Bad = anyPain ; start the good - bad trees.

anyPain = PainL o PainR

fePain=fePainhL o fePainhR o fePainlL o fePainlR
knPain=knPainhL o knPainhR o knPainlL o knPainlR
hiPain=hiPainhL o hiPainhR o hiPainlL o hi-PainlR
elPain=elPainhL o elPainhR o elPainlL o elPainlR
arPain = arPainL o arPainR
;
PainL=fePainL o knPainL o hiPainL o elPainL o arPainL
PainR=fePainR o knPainR o hiPainR o elPainR o arPainR

This is how you collect a large network of similar data. You can use it in its parts or whole.

I reach a means of goal setting now. I want to increase Goodness which means adding to Good or taking away Bad. I am now in the inner layer of the brain where sensors are combined into object concepts.

First, I detect objects. From vision, I define an object as anything that covers two sensors or has equal inputs at the same time to two separated sensors.

While detecting an object, I am collecting attributes of the object. Concepts are a PNode property tree of attributes, and will generally be a numeric code that is related to the sum of its attributes.
(In English grammar, objects are nouns and attributes are adjectives. The arithmetic is like:

```
ThisNoun = SomeQualifier + SomeSmallerNoun
Man      = rational      + animal
```

We can establish consciousness by providing HalStreams that collect "what I am doing" objects. Tree notation can be used here to for illustration. They can be expanded for construction. (See Tree Systems)

LegStatusL=hiBendingL o knBendingL o feBendingL
LegStatusR=hiBendingR o knBendingR o feBendingR)

ArmStatusL=arRotatingL o arLiftingL o arPainL
ArmStatusR=arRotatingR o arLiftingR o arPAinR

WhatDoing=walking o sitting o standing o peeing o
drinking o speaking o hearing o seeing o hatouching

WhatDone = walked o sat o stood o peed o drunk o seen o hatouched

Seeing and seen should be collected from vision objects.
Hearing and heard should be collected from hearing objects.

All this is collected into now and just past. Note that now flows into just past which flows into past just like a single Hal stream.

This is the first level of code for Big Al. The second level will provide trees for goals we already have. Walk, stand and sit are all open and ready for does and don'ts. This level will start providing personality. How many levels of code are there? Until 1994 we could not write the first level. Who thinks they know how to write the second level, leaving sockets for the third level?

[to be continued]

1. To Close

These applications are my attempts to show the way. At the same time, they show my ignorance. Please, dear reader, apply this Hal stream math to your interests. This is why I wrote the book. As you have seen, I make tools for you to make robots, animachines, appliances, or things we have not imagined yet. This is the beginning, the machine language stage of development. Machine language requires writing down every HalNode. We will have compilers to do that for us someday. We will write goals and wishes, and the compiler will create the HalNode list. Still much later, our compiler will assemble the hardware. We will go directly from goals and wishes to hardware.

When Claude Shannon married Boolean algebra to switches, he was not required to build the computers that resulted. If Claude had microcontrollers available to him then, he would have put arithmetic to them just as I have done. Here I have married arithmetic to HalNodes and cables and I have to build Robots in addition.

It is time to start thinking about machines with consciousness and emotion. Of course, should I die, this might molder for another two hundred years. I was in a unique configuration to discover this. When I did (3/26/1994), it all became obvious and I never could understand why it was so hard to explain to people. After all this started in the 1700's with the first mechanical automatons. Now we can make them properly, and proceed to make ourselves which is the only way we can understand how we are made.

1. Appendix 1 Floating point HalStreams

To make real HalStreams, borrow from the computer the notion of floating point numbers. Then make integer to float from sensors and float to integer to motors. All nodes then do floating point arithmetic. Multiplication and division can be added to the operation set. (Now any function can be added as a node.)

Hal stream size, w will have to increase to handle the exponents while keeping the dynamic range.

This system then will do any mathematical computation for curves in real time, providing a machine way to do proofs. Now we all are forced to use a cleaner syntax for writing math.

1. Appendix 2 Cellular Automata

Since Steven Wolfram's huge book "A New Kind of Science' is out, I must comment about cellular automata. The big fault that lies beneath any computer program, is that it belongs to the computer. There is no way to take it outside. The minor fault is that the computer is a linear machine, a machine that writes with one point. Cellular automata are all computer programs. They are however, HalTrees if you consider inputs and outputs. Generally, in the computer, a cell has one to eight neighbors. The computer program sweeps past each cell and produces its output. There is a sequence here that is often forgotten. (What is forgotten is the linear computer.)

In the computer, dimension one cells are c[i] where i is from 0 to N. The computation is c[i] = f(c[i-1]). In two dimensional cellular systems the cell is c[i,j] and the computation is c[i,j] = f(c[i-1,j-1]). About the maximum number of neighbors the cell can have is eight. Then c[i,j,k,l,m,n,o,p] is the cell. Each cell has one output, its own value, but the output is split eight ways. This is true no matter what the dimension. In the computer, the cell is updated by sweeping through all the subscripts. This means that each cell is updated all by itself every time while every other cell is inactive. Commonly, cellular automata are started with one cell c[0] and the other cells are grown from some rule. There was never the idea of a fixed array of cells that computed. The idea was to grow cells by repeating some rule.

A common out of the computer illustration of cellular automata is the crowd at a football game with colored cards that are displayed by some rule. Even this is different from cellular automata in the computer. Here is a fixed array of cells, displaying data by rule. Here each cell does its own processing and the overall display is done simultaneously by all cells at the same time.

To really take cellular automata out of the computer we have to use HalTrees. Each cell then becomes a one to eight input HalTree, from HalTree{i} to HalTree{i,j,k,l,n,n,o,p}.

With HalTrees we have a fixed array of cells, now nodes, which compute according to the rule in each node. This is completely upside down from cellular automata.

1. The Author

I am Harold L. Reed

Email is: hlreed@halbrain.com
Visit my website at http://www.halbrain.com

1. References and Notes

Books, sorted by author name

Ashby, W. Ross, Design for a Brain, Wiley & Sons, 1960
Stability. The homeostat. Cybernetics. Early IF -THEN not adequate discovery. This started control systems. No one paid attention to the limitations. Ashby showed that IF-THEN logic could not scale, which is why all current robots are four function machines. Add the fifth function and it all collapses.

Albus, James S., Brains, Behavior, and Robotics, BYTE/McGraw Hill, 1981
Actually proposes a model, the CAMAC. Problems were, inputs had weights and output was binary. Vector representation of brain codes is good, but vectors can be rewritten as HalStreams.

Braitenberg, Valentino, Vehicles, The MIT Press, 1984
This little book was written up in Scientific American. His Vehicles are Robots. His vehicles have sensors and motors. When he connects sensors directly to motors he is fine. But then he defaults to logic and magic and begins to wander away.

Cardwell, Donald, The Norton History of Technology, W.W. Norton & Company, 1995
A good history of technology in context with general history. He points out in several places that new technology is always produced by outsiders. I would extend this to all new ideas.

Heiserman, David L., Robot Intelligence with experiments
Tab Books, Inc. 1981

Some TRS-80 programs illustrating some ideas on robot intelligence in the scheme of AI.

Kelly, Kevin, Out of Control, Addison-Wesley, 1995
Mr. Kelly understands the difference between a Von Neumann Computer and a Cybernetic control system. This book covers everything touched by chaos and complexity with the new attitude that requires.

Kelso, J. A. Scott, Dynamic Patterns, The MIT Press, 1995
Self-organization and patterns. No mechanism yet.

Kline, Morris, Mathematics and the Search for Knowledge, Oxford University Press, 1985
What mathematics reveals about nature.

Kosko, Bart, Fuzzy Thinking, Hyperion, 1993
A passionate promotion of fuzzy logic. I use his fuzzy thermostat as a counter example.

Levenson, Thompson, Measure for Measure, Simon & Schuster, 1994
"A Musical History of Science." This is a beautiful essay on science, from the Pythagorean beginnings.

Loyd, Seth, Programming the Universe, Alfred A. Knopf
2006
The universe as a quantum computer. Don't know about the quantum part, but it surely computes.

Mandelbrot, Benoit B, The Fractal Geometry of Nature, W.H. Freeman and Company, 1977,1983
This is the book that told us the world was fractal. Before that we did not think about it because we could not see it.

McNiel, Daniel and Freiberger, Paul, Fuzzy Logic, Simon & Schuster, 1993
Story of fuzzy development.

Raphael, Bertram, The Thinking Computer, W.H. Freeman and Company, 1976
History of AI up to 1976, which is far enough.

Reed, Harold L., Brains for Machines/Machines for Brains, Nova Science Publishers, Inc., 1996
HalNodes and algebra are developed here in a story of discovery. Looking for the least brain function. Has been republished as Comparison and Choice.

Reed, Harold L., From Electric Numbers to Hal Trees, Creatspace, 2009 The mathematics of Hal Trees.

Reed, Harold L. Some Short Proofs of Fermat's Last Theorem an application of Hal Algebra.

Rosheim, Mark E., Robot Evolution, John Wiley & Sons, 1994
A good history and commentary on "Anthrobots," manlike robots, by a practitioner in the field of robotics design.

Schroeder, Manfred, Fractals, Chaos, Power Laws, W.H. Freeman and Company, 1991
Good stuff on self similarity and scale invariance, which I use eagerly.

Von Neumann, John, The Computer and the Brain, Yale University Press, 1958
This is an unfinished presentation he was working on when he died. He had to do this without words like "programs, software, registers, Index, Loops" and so on. Computer parts were "organs".

1. Index

A

B

C

D

F

G

H

I

L

M

N

O

P

R

S

T

V

W

X

www.ingramcontent.com/pod-product-compliance
Lightning Source LLC
Chambersburg PA
CBHW071359050326
40689CB00010B/1689

* 9 7 8 1 4 4 9 5 9 9 5 4 6 *